HENRY GOTCH SCHOOLS

1939 - 2009

JOHN SELLERS

ISBN: 9780956544667

Printed by
CTB Print & Design Ltd
Harcourt Street
Kettering
Northants
NN16 0RS

Published by
Armadillo Design & Print
Unit 10, Stafford Place
Moulton Park
Northanmpton
NN3 6NN

I WOULD LIKE TO THANK EVERYONE WHO HAS
CONTRIBUTED TO THE MAKING OF THIS BOOK,
CONTRIBUTIONS HAVE COME FROM ALL AROUND THE
GLOBE. SPECIAL THANKS TO IRENE BITHRAY AND PAT
BUSSEY FOR ALLOWING ME TO USE PHOTOGRAPHS
AND MATERIAL FROM THEIR PRIVATE COLLECTIONS.
FOR ME PERSONALLY, IT HAS BEEN A LABOUR OF LOVE,
12 YEARS OF MY LIFE WAS SPENT AT HENRY GOTCH
SCHOOLS, NURSERY, INFANTS, JUNIORS AND
SECONDARY MODERN 1947 - 1959. I HOPE EVERYONE
WHO READS IT, ENJOYS IT, AND IT BRINGS BACK
MEMORIES, HAPPY AND SAD, OF TIMES GONE BY. THE
AUTHOR / PUBLISHER GRATEFULLY ACKNOWLEDGES
PERMISSION GRANTED TO REPRODUCE COPYRIGHT
MATERIAL IN THIS BOOK, EVERY EFFORT HAS BEEN
MADE TO CONTACT COPYRIGHT HOLDERS, IF ANY. IF
CORRECTIONS ARE NEEDED, THE AUTHOR / PUBLISHER
WILL GRATEFULLY INCORPORATE THEM IN FUTURE
EDITIONS.

"MY FAVOURITE PHOTOGRAPH"

THIS BOOK IS DEDICATED TO THE MEMORY OF MY LATE WIFE LESLEY
1947 - 2004

LATEST WORD IN SCHOOL CONSTRUCTION

Interesting Details About Kettering's Newest Acquisition.

THE HENRY GOTCH SCHOOLS.

Here is seen Kettering's new schools, the Henry Gotch Schools in Windmill-avenue, which will be formally opened by Mr. Kenneth M. Lindsay, M.P., Parliamentary Secretary to the Board of Education, on June 30th. The junior department of the school was opened for use on Tuesday, when the summer term began in Kettering schools; the infants' department will not be ready until about June 5th.

KETTERING'S new £46,000 Henry Gotch Schools in Windmill-avenue, the Junior Department of which was opened for use on Tuesday, embodies the latest ideas in school building and development.

Among the modern features of the school, which will appeal to the popular imagination are the electrically controlled heating apparatus and the electric "buzzers", which have supplanted the traditional school bell.

Seated at his desk the head teacher in each department—junior and infants—of the school, will be able, by pressing a lever, to control the amount of finely ground coal which is being automatically fed into the boilers of the heating system.

Thus, without any other human agency he will control the temperature of the school.

Buzzer Instead of Bell.

Equally simple will be the task of the head teacher when playtime is over. He will simply press a button working the "buzzers," which recall the scholars to work.

From an educational point of view the most interesting feature of the school is that the infants' department has a nursery section.

Subway for Scholars.

Equally novel will be the fact that the school will be approached by a subway under Windmill-avenue. This subway, designed to eliminate the danger to the children of crossing this busy road, opens direct into the school grounds, and is believed to be the first in the country to be built exclusively for a school. The subway will be completed early in June, when the infants department of the school will be ready for use. The school will be formally opened on June 30th by Sir Kenneth M. Lindsay, M.P. Parliamentary Secretary of the Board of Education.

History of the Undertaking.

It was in July, 1934, that the local authority first considered erecting a school in Windmill-avenue, but it was not until March, 1936, that the statutory notice to proceed with the scheme was issued. Mr. J. T. Blackwell, the architect, was instructed to repare plans for the school and these were submitted to the Board of Education in July, 1936. In November, 1936, the site, comprising over 18 acres, was acquired for £7,060, and the idea of a subway was suggested in the same month.

Tenders for the new school were invited in August, 1937, and in October the tender of Messrs. H. C. Janes, Ltd., Luton, was accepted for £39,064. Final approval of the Government was given, and the contractors commenced work in June, 1938. In December, 1937, it was decided that the school should be called the "Henry Gotch Schools," to commemorate the services of Mr. H. G. Gotch to education.

For the construction of the subway the tender of £2,161, submitted by the Works Department of Kettering Borough Council, was accepted in December, 1938.

Two paintings of Mr. G. Harrison, the well-known Kettering artist, have been generously given to hang in the hall of the two departments of the school.

The Schools Described.

The following description of the school has been supplied to the "Kettering Leader" by the architect, Mr. J. T. Blackwell, and the secretary to Kettering Education Committee (Mr. E. J. Loasby):

The Henry Gotch Schools comprise two separate blocks of buildings—that to the north of the approach road from the Windmill-avenue, being a Junior School to accommodate 384 scholars in eight classrooms, desked for 48 pupils in each. Two of the rooms are fitted and equipped so as to afford facilities for teaching practical subjects.

The block on the south side of the approach road is an Infants' School, with complete Nursery School accommodation combined. The Infants' School provides for 336 scholars in seven classrooms, and the Nursery School provides for 40 babies, the nursery accommodation being situated on the south side of the building, with separate entrance and playground.

The nursery block is self-contained, with generous cloakroom, bathing and sanitary accommodation, blanket and bed store, laundry, kitchen, larder, and lobby on the north side of the school, leading into the internal open court. This lobby also gives access to the largest of the classrooms, which is to be seated with little tables and chairs and is to serve as a dining room for infants whose parents arrange for their children to stay for a midday meal.

Each school has a large assembly hall, lighted and ventilated on both sides, and whilst being completely isolated from the teaching rooms, opens direct on to the glazed corridors which give access to the verandahs round which the classrooms are planned. The head teacher's room in each school is situated so that it commands a view of all the classrooms, and the staff rooms are planned so as to overlook the playgrounds and the playing field. A clinic is provided in the Infants' School, which will serve the Junior School also, with direct access.

Careful Planning.

Long and careful thought has been given to the planning of these schools, both of which have been grouped round large open courts so that every classroom in both schools has a southern aspect. Moreover, the directness of the layout of the buildings generally, and the juxtaposition of the separate units is so noticeable as to invite favourable comments from experts. A further noticeable feature of the scheme is that both schools are of the open-air type, but wisely, provision has been made on this open site for closing the corridors in rough and boisterous weather.

The buildings generally, have been kept severe and simple in design, and are faced outside with Tucker's multi-red facing bricks, and the roofs covered with Tucker's tiles.

Steel windows and folding doors have been used throughout for lighting purposes.

The heating throughout is from low pressure hot water twin boilers, interchanging, in each basements, and are fed by automatic stokers, as well as the boilers supplying the hot water services.

Special care has been given to the scheme of decorations, so as to secure a cheerful and restful result.

A caretaker's house has been provided on the site, overlooking the approaches as well as the playing fields.

ORDER OF PROCEEDINGS.

Chairman: ALDERMAN H. MARTIN, J.P.
(Chairman of Education Committee).

1. Chairman's Introductory Remarks.

2. KENNETH LINDSAY, ESQ., M.P., will declare the School open.

3. Presentations to KENNETH LINDSAY, ESQ., M.P., by J. T. BLACKWELL, ESQ., Architect, and by a Scholar of the Infants' School.

4. Vote of thanks to KENNETH LINDSAY, ESQ., M.P., to be
   (a) *Proposed by* His Worship the Mayor (ALDERMAN J. HAYNES, J.P.).
   (b) *Seconded by* ALDERMAN A. A. THORNTON, C.C.

5. Vote of Thanks to Chairman to be
   (a) *Proposed by* MISS S. GREEN.
   (b) *Seconded by* G. HARRISON, ESQ.

6. Unveiling of Commemoration Tablet by HIS WORSHIP THE MAYOR.

7. Formal Opening of School Subway by COUNCILLOR W. H. SUMPTER *(Chairman of Estates and Buildings Committee).*

TEA will be served in the Infants' Hall immediately after the Ceremony. Afterwards, Guests are invited to inspect the School Buildings.

BOROUGH OF KETTERING
EDUCATION COMMITTEE

PROGRESSIO ET CONCORDIA

The OFFICIAL OPENING *of the*
HENRY GOTCH COUNCIL SCHOOL

BY

KENNETH M. LINDSAY, ESQ., M.P.,
Parliamentary Secretary of the Board of Education.

FRIDAY, 30TH JUNE, 1939,
at 2-30 p.m.

HENRY GOTCH SCHOOL.

IT was in July, 1934, that the Education Committee first considered the acquisition of a site in Windmill Avenue for the erection of a new School to serve the rapidly growing area known as the Piper's Hill Estate.

It was not until March, 1936, that Statutory Notice to proceed with the proposal was issued, and at the same time Mr. J. T. Blackwell was instructed to prepare sketch plans for a school for Juniors and Infants.

In July, 1936, sketch plans were submitted to the Board of Education.

In November, 1936, the site in Windmill Avenue was secured, comprising a little over 18 acres at a cost of £7,060.

In November, 1936, the suggestion was made that a Subway should be constructed to give access to the School without the necessity of children crossing Windmill Avenue.

Tenders for the erection of the School were invited in August, 1937, and at the end of October the tender of Messrs. H. C. Janes Ltd., of Luton, amounting to the sum of £39,064 10s. 1d. was accepted.

On the 15th December, 1937, the approval of the Board of Education was given to the whole Scheme.

It was in December, 1937, that the Authority decided to commemorate the services of Mr. Henry Gale Gotch by naming the School "The Henry Gotch Council School."

The contractors commenced work on the site in January, 1938.

On the 5th December, 1938, the Tender of the Corporation Works Department for the construction of the Subway to the School, amounting to £2,160 15s. 1d., was accepted.

THE SCHOOL BUILDING.

THE Schools comprise two separate blocks of buildings—that to the north of the approach road from the Windmill Avenue, being a Junior School to accommodate 384 scholars in eight classrooms, desked for 48 pupils in each. Two of the rooms are fitted and equipped so as to afford facilities for teaching practical subjects.

The block on the south side of the approach road is an Infants' School, with complete Nursery School accommodation combined. The Infants' School provides for 336 scholars in seven classrooms, and the Nursery School provides for 40 babies, the Nursery accommodation being situated on the south side of the building, with a separate entrance and playground.

The Nursery block is self-contained, with generous cloakroom, bathing and sanitary accommodation, blanket and bed store, laundry, kitchen, larder, and lobby on the north side of the School, leading into the internal open court. This lobby also gives access to the largest of the classrooms, which is to be seated with little tables and chairs and is to serve as a dining room for infants whose parents arrange for their children to stay for a mid-day meal.

Each School has a large assembly hall, lighted and ventilated on both sides, and whilst being completely isolated from the teaching rooms, opens direct on to the glazed corridors which give access to the verandahs round which the classrooms are planned. The head teachers' room in each School is situated so that it commands a view of all the classrooms, and the staffrooms are planned so as to overlook the playgrounds and the playing-field.

A clinic is provided in the Infants' School, which will serve the Junior School also, with direct access.

HENRY GALE GOTCH.

Biographical Notes.

H.G.Cotch was born on October 8th, 1848, at Jasmine House, which stands at the junction of Lower Street and Tanners' Lane, close to the Post Office.

He was the eldest child of Thomas Henry Gotch, and one of four brothers, two of whom, John Alfred, the Architect-Antiquarian, and Thomas Cooper, the Artist, made the name of Gotch widely known through their eminence in their respective professions.

The family were originally Yeoman farmers, and trace their direct descent back to Hugh Gotch of East Langton, just over the border in Leicestershire. On the distaff side they are descended from John Okey, a prominent Colonel of Horse in the Parliamentarian Army; he was executed in 1662.

The family moved to Kettering about 1745, when H.G.'s great-great-grandfather married a Rothwell girl and lived for a time at Cherry Hall, now little more than a cottage on the Rockingham Road, just beyond the turning to Glendon.

His son moved into Kettering, and resided for a few years where the Northamptonshire Union Bank used to stand in the High Street, and was one of the earliest, if not the first boot manufacturer in Kettering, under the title of Thomas Gotch & John Cobb (1786). This firm subsequently became T.H.Gotch & Sons, H.G. being one of the latter, and carried on for more than a century. He bought Chesham House in 1793, and built the factory which used to adjoin the House on the town side; it was here that Henry Gale started work after he left the Grammar School in 1864 or 5.

It was also in the same factory that William Carey, the Baptist Missionary, spoilt so much leather that H.G.'s grandfather paid him 10/- a week to go on with his bible studies instead, and always considered it the best investment he had ever made!

Of Henry Gotch's schooldays little is known; but his brother Davis always spoke very enthusiastically of the excellent instruction they received from Mr. ? Wilkinson, the headmaster and both brothers were above the usual standard in mathematics, a faculty probably inherited from their father, Thomas Henry, who wrote one of the early books published on logarithms.

He was almost certainly a quiet, rather reserved boy, a trait which characterized him throughout his life; not particularly enthusiastic as regards games, though he played Rugby football on the Ground in Green Lane in the seventies. From 1871-1888 or so he lived at Chesham House as a bachelor, and developed three hobbies, two of which he adhered to through most of his life. They were Music, Mountaineering and Astronomy. The latter interest he shared with his father who had an enormous telescope housed in a wooden shed in Chesham House Garden, which was a source of awe and wonder to the writer for many years.

His musical ability derived chiefly from his mother, many evenings being spent in playing family quartets, Henry's instrument being the 'cello, though he was also a fluatist of no mean ability. From these early efforts he must have obtained his knowledge of music which resulted in his becoming conductor of the Kettering Choral Society from 1880 - 1888 or so, when he left Kettering for a few years, on the dissolution of the business of T.H.Gotch & Sons.

In 1911 he bought the old family home, Chesham House, and made considerable improvements, demolishing the old factory, except for that part which is now the Kitchen and best bedroom; and he remained there until 1921, when he moved to Angus House in the Headlands, and lived there for the rest of his days.

Politically he was an unobtrusive but ardent liberal, and was Hon. Treasurer of the party association for many years, from the time of Channing to the sad days of its decline, which he much deplored, believing that it would not be conducive to the good of the nation, and opinion shared by many of varying political faiths.

A man's social assets are best known to those of his own generation, but I think his peers would have assessed him as a "gilt-edged security" at any social function. Punctiliously courteous, unassumingly self-confident, a somewhat slow starter conversationally, but good to listen to when on a subject he knew - and these were considerable in number. He had the habit of sitting back, fingers together listening to others; and would then unexpectedly throw into the company a gem of rather dry subtle wit. As a public speaker he was mellow rather than fluent, not amusing, but witty, eulogistic and sparing of criticism.

The reserve inherent in his character assuredly covered a depth of feeling both human and religious: with a lover of mountains and children it could hardly be otherwise: but his deeper thoughts were rarely exhibited for the approval or criticism of others. A loyal husband, a strict but unrestrictive father: he was, I believe, at his happiest when in the company of either or all of his brothers, or his sister Jessie.

So far I have dealt only with the background and character of the man after whom the HENRY GALE GOTCH school was named, and have not referred to the long years of public service in the cause of education which brought him this tribute from his fellow citizens.

His interest in education was stimulated by the conditions prevalent in the sixties, when the only schools were those supported and fostered by religious denominations, and at a time when the only education some children received was gained at the Sunday Schools. Noncomformists especially felt this handicap, and the Gotch family, being dissenters, were deeply interested in education, and consequently in the British School, which was undenominational.

H.G. was barely 21 when he was appointed Secretary to the trustees of the school, to which was added six years later the position of Treasurer. He was succeeded by his brother Alfred in 1879, in order that he might accept the position of Chairman to the Governing Body of the Grammar School, which he relinquished when he left Kettering in 1888.

The School Board which existed between 1890 and 1903, of which Davis Gotch was the only Chairman, was dissolved soon after H.G. returned to the town. The control of education passed to the Urban District Council, and it was not by chance that H.G. was encouraged to become a member of the Council and immediately appointed the first Chairman of the Education Committee in 1903, of which he remained an active member until his retirement in 1934. His services on the council led to his becoming its Chairman - equivalent to Mayor - in 1906, and later to his election to the County Council. Here again his knowledge of educational matters were appreciated, and for many years he was on the County Committee dealing with Secondary Education. Such faithful service was rewarded by Aldermanic honours, and by his elevation to the bench of Magistrates as a J.P.

Such, in brief outline, were the services given by H.G. to his native town and county in the cause of education.

From the age of 20 until he was 85 his interest never flagged; and only consciousness of failing faculties caused him to resign this work to which he had devoted so many years.

It was with humbleness that he accepted the honour conferred on him by the town in 1929, and later in that year he passed away on July 26th, aged 90.

A man of sound judgement and upright intentions held in high esteem by his fellows and in sincere affection by his relatives.

LAURENCE. M. GOTCH.

HENRY GOTCH

DEEBLE ROAD

WINDMILL AVENUE

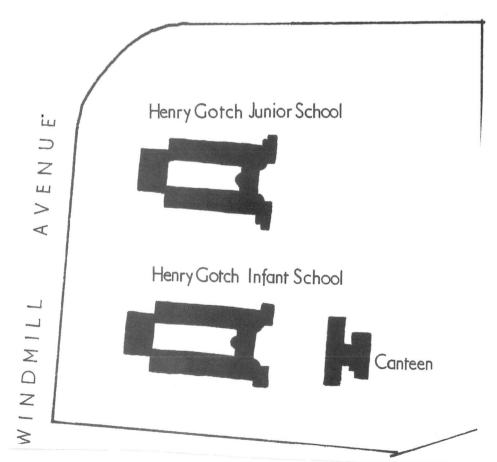

Henry Gotch Junior School

Henry Gotch Infant School

Canteen

1939

Long and careful thought has been given to the planning of these schools, both of which have been grouped round large open courts so that every classroom in both schools has a southern aspect. Moreover, the directness of the layout of the buildings generally, and the juxtaposition of the separate units is so noticeable as to invite favourable comments from experts. A further noticeable feature of the scheme is that both schools are of the open-air type, but wisely, provision has been made on this open site, for closing the corridors in rough and boisterous weather.

The buildings generally have been kept severe and simple in design, and are faced outside with Tucker's Multi-red facing bricks, and the roofs covered with Tucker's tiles.

Steel windows and folding-doors have been used throughout for lighting purposes.

The heating throughout is from low pressure hot water twin boilers, interchanging, in each basement, and are fed by automatic stokers, as well as the boilers supplying the hot water services.

Special care has been given to the scheme of decorations, so as to secure a cheerful and restful result.

A caretaker's house has been provided on the site, overlooking the approaches as well as the playing-fields.

Messrs. H. C. Janes, Ltd., of Luton, the General Contractors, have worked with the following sub-contractors who have carried out the work on their behalf :—

Heating (Infants' School)	Messrs. W. Freer, Ltd., Leicester.
„ (Junior School) -	Messrs. S. Booth Horrocks & Sons, Ltd., Kettering.
Plumbing - - - -	Messrs. A. G. Miller, Ltd., Kettering.

1 Our First Admissions

Admission Number	Date of Admission Day / Mth / Year	Date of Re-Admission Day / Mth / Year	NAME IN FULL (Surname First)	Evidence of Date of Birth*	Date of Birth Day / Mth / Year	ADDRESS	NAME OF PARENT OR GUARDIAN
1.	5 6 39		Sykes Peter Frederick		1 2 31	1, Pine Road	Arthur
2.	5 6 39		Sanders Cornelius Alfred Edward		1 2 31	25A, Windmill Avenue	Alfred Edwo
3.	5 6 39		Dawkins Arthur William		6 2 31	47, Oak Road	William
4.	5 6 39		Moore Anthony Frank		6 3 31	131, St. Mary's Rd.	Leslie Painter
5.	5 6 39		West Colin John		6 3 31	33, East Av.	Arthur
6.	5 6 39		Thompson Barrie Howard		12 3 31	18, Fir Road	Albert Edwar
7.	5 6 39		Tirrell Geoffrey Thomas		1 4 31	81, Linden Av.	Ralph.
8.	5 6 39		York Donald Frederick		16 4 31	24, Pine Rd.	Frederick Hare
9.	5 6 39		Stapleton Roy William.		25 4 31	108, St. Mary's Rd	Horace
10.	6 6 39		Mitchell Arthur William Jeffcoat		30 4 31	15, Windmill Av.	William

C.B. Certificate: Dr's Certificate: etc.

Our First Evacuees Arrive

501	20 8 40				19 8 33	67, The Ovall		13 Ashmount ... NW.2
502	20 8 40				19 -1 34	21, Valley Walk		72 Eastcheap go. EC1.
50?	20 8 40				2 3 34	14, Oak Rd.		31, Clapham ... E.C.1.
504	20 8 40				3 6 34	53, Belvedere Rd		33 ... Burgh St. EC1

IN MEMORIAM

HENRY GALE GOTCH

1848-1939

HENRY GALE GOTCH, who died on July 26, 1939, was elected to this Club in 1876, being proposed by Edward Whymper and seconded by C. E. Mathews. Nearly all his chief expeditions took place before his marriage in 1889, but his interest in the mountains continued throughout his life and was transmitted to his children. He was one of the founders of the Climbers' Club, of which his son was for a number of years Honorary Secretary. An excellent account of his attempt upon La Meije in 1876, with Alexandre Tournier and Henri Dévouassoud, is contained in *A.J.* 8. 177 *sqq.* It was characteristic of him that he retained a close friendship with many guides who had accompanied him on the mountains. His son writes : 'His conversation turned continually to guides. I should not be surprised if Joseph Imboden were his closest friend. They never missed meeting if my father were in Switzerland, and knew each other so well that they never used the customary handshake, but just grinned at each other and administered a tap on the shoulder.'

Besides being a Justice of the Peace for Northamptonshire, Gotch was busy with much public service, especially in the interests of education, and in return for over seventy years of such service in his leisure life his name is commemorated in the Henry Gotch School at Kettering, which was opened on June 30, 1939—a unique distinction in his county. He was also a skilled and sympathetic musician, acting as conductor of the Kettering Choral Society for about fifty years.

(From notes supplied by Mr. M. S. GOTCH.)

In Memoriam

HENRY GALE GOTCH

1848-1939

Reprinted from 'THE ALPINE JOURNAL,' November 1940

Printed by

SPOTTISWOODE, BALLANTYNE & CO, LTD., NEW-STREET SQ., E.C. 4

1940

18th April 1939
Junior school opens.
195 children on roll.

15th May 1939
First ARP (Air Raid Precautions) safety trenches are dug by the Junior School. The children practise getting into them quickly, every day, instead of P.E.

31st August 1939
School closes early so the building can be used as an evacuation centre.

September 1939
School operates a 2 shift system. Kettering children use classrooms in morning and hall or fields in afternoon. London children do the opposite.

20th November 1939
School closes at sunset so children and staff can get home safely in the blackout.

Kettering Urban District Education Committee

E. 1.

28th May, 1929.

Dear Sir,

I beg to inform you that the Committee have decided to empower you to administer corporal punishment in accordance with the Regulations. You will be supplied with Punishment Book and cane in due course.

Yours faithfully,

Secretary to the Committee.

Mr. E. R. Corby,
Stamford Road Mixed School,
Kettering.

Henry Gotch Infant and Junior School 1940-47. Staff I remember well are Miss Tate who wore dresses made of crepe (I thought they were paper). Mr. Birtwhistle and Mr. Corby both well respected Headmasters. Miss Wildman - her hair braided into plaits round her ears. Miss Chaston patiently trying to teach me subtraction. Miss Rees, a very firey lady but fair. Mr. Arnold and Ted, the caretakers bringing the crates of small bottles of milk, (ice cold in winter, tepid and smelly in summer) to each class.

B-cause of sleep lost during air raids the infants were expected to rest in the ^ ernoon. Camp beds were erected in the corridors. Not many of us slept but I remember one girl sleeping through the afternoon and having to be woken to go home!

We had regular air raid drills to the shelters constructed opposite the Junior School, parallel with Deeble Road.

During this time my brother contracted diphtheria. My teacher was notified. I was to be excluded from school. I must have been a happy pupil because I hid in the cloakroom and was bribed by Mr. Arnold with 6d and a ride on his bicycle to go home.

For minor disobediences we were sent to stand under the clock outside the Headmaster's room.

I remember being bell monitor, the bell pushes were in the Headmaster's room and it was an honour to press the bells for playtime, home time etc.

Jean Bridgstock
(nee Crane)

HENRY GOTCH - THE SCHOOL WITH THE TUNNEL - Shirley Hockridge (nee Mayers) '940

I was just 5 years old when the Henry Gotch School opened. I lived in Oak Road and could see the school from my house.

My mother took me into the Infants section, I had started my Nursery schooling at Avondale Road school, so I was too old to go into the Nursery, but I used to see the little beds out in the corridor that were used for the children in the Nursery to have a sleep every afternoon Everything was so new and modern, it was the most modern school in the town and we were so lucky to have a tunnel to go under, to get into the school, which meant we did not have to cross the road. If a teacher caught you crossing the road then you got a good telling off and had to stand under the clock during playtime as punishment.

I moved through the Infants and into the Junior school, by this time the war was on, I didn't realise how terrible this was, but I remember a lot of evacuees came to Kettering from London and remember them crying with their gas masks hanging round their necks as they were handed to local people to be looked after. A lot of those evacuees still keep in touch with the families that took them in.

They started coming to Henry Gotch and it made such a difference that for a long time we only went to school for half days, one week mornings the next afternoons, on a rota basis.

Where the Senior School is now that is where the underground air raid shelters were situated and at weekends we would go down and play over the shelters, there were manholes that could be lifted up and you then climbed down the metal ladders leading down into the shelter corridors in which seats and bunks were left for us should there be an air raid. I remember having to go down on two occasions when there was an air raid, while in the winter we would use the run ways into the shelters as slides and to sledge down when it snowed.

We didn't have the swimming pool that is in the Junior school now, but we had our Sports Day and trips out into the country for nature days as the Ise Village estate was all fields.

OH! HAPPY HENRY GOTCH SCHOOLDAYS   1940

by Irene Rithray (nee Laux)

Henry Gotch Junior was the only school I chose and it was my happiest.

I was placed in Miss Wildman's class. I still have and use a book about trees and shrubs that she gave me as a first prize for collecting wild flowers.

Miss Lenton, the art and craft teacher, was quite a character. She used to tuck her handkerchief in her knickers. One day we met her, handkerchief dangling below her long skirt, in the corridor. A friend bravely approached her and said, "Miss Lenton your handkerchief is showing". Miss Lenton immediately grasped it, lifted her skirt and deposited it back into her knickers, before our startled gazes.

It was wartime and everyone was exhorted to "Dig for Victory". The central quadrangle was turned into a garden. My friend Rita Moore and I were given the task of watering the tomatoes daily during the last period. We were told to use the teachers kettle, dipping it into the water butt, which contained many dead and alive insects (on one occasion there was a dead blackbird). We did this for several weeks until a horrified teacher noticed. After that we had to borrow large enamel jugs from Miss Lenton.

One day we arrived at school only to discover Canadian soldiers camped on the spare ground on the corner of Windmill Avenue and, what is now, Deeble Road. We walked among the tents until Mr Birtwhistle, our well-respected and liked Headmaster, forbade us. On one occasion a soldier threw a large lump of fat on to 'our' fence. The greasy mark stayed there for years.

Mr other memories include:-

Going into damp, cold shelters clutching my tin of sweets, kept in my desk for emergencies.
Running home early as a local town was being bombed
Going for nature walks and collecting rose-hip berries which we were told would be turned into syrup
Getting tadpoles from the gentle Ise brook
Making bamboo pipes and pretending I had all the holes for a photograph, which I still have
Being in the Hall, well spaced, and singing rousing patriotic songs, ignoring a slight commotion on my right (as we had been firmly instructed) only to find out later that my neighbour had been carried out by the staff as she had fainted
Having all the panes of glass criss-crossed with tape to prevent glass flying if there was a bomb. I hated it as it cut out a lot of light
Going under the tunnel (unnecessary as we then had to cross the road at a further point) under the watchful eyes of the teachers, who reprimanded those children who should have used the tunnel and tried to avoid doing so.

1ST CLASS PHOTO, SPRING 1940

20th June 1940
The Government
considers using the
building as a military
hospital.

3rd & 4th December 1940
The children spend nearly
an hour each day in the
trenches because of an
air raid.

CLASS 4A, HENRY GOTCH JUNIOR SCHOOL, 1942.
HANDMADE BAMBOO PIPES

JANUARY 1941

MADE OWN INSTRUMENTS: FORMED OWN BAND.

Little Music Lovers of Kettering School.

PRACTISING the arts of peace in time of war, under the guidance of their head teacher, Mr D P Birtwisle and his senior assistant Mr E R Corby the children of the Henry Gotch Junior School, Kettering, have formed their own pipe band and made their own pipes.

A representative of this journal was entertained at the simple beauty of the bending pipes as the young musicians played "The First Noel".

The children are very enthusiastic, and fashion their pipes from pieces of thick bamboo cane. Shortening them until the right pitch is obtained, and then making holes in the tube and tuning them to the notes of the scale.

At first they all learn one straightforward tune. They take the pipes home with them to practise, and soon learn to play, helped by bands and orchestras on the wireless.

They gave a demonstration to one of our reporters on Friday. One lad played "Over the Rainbow," another "There'll Always be an England."

This school is one of a few in the country that has taken up this idea of having its own pipe band. Introduced by Mr. Corby, the scheme helps to develop the musical knowledge and appreciation of the children.

If a child cannot sing as is the case with many, he or she can usually learn to play a simple musical instrument, and thus develop a liking for all types of music in the words of Mr. Corby. They can soon tell when a note is sharp or flat.

Here are some of the young music enjoyers of the Henry Gotch School playing a tune on the recorder like pipes they have fashioned themselves.

"MEMORIES"

by Sheila Clipston (nee Tooke) (1942 - 49)

After moving down from London I started in the Nursery school. I remember my Mickey Mouse gas mask and using the school air raid shelter.

Afternoon naps on canvas beds in the school corridor, covered by grey blankets with animal motifs on. I remember being in a school concert where one of the props were real buns and someone stole mine (the culprit shall be nameless!)

Unfortunately, my father was killed in Tobruk in 1942, but the Headmistress of the Infant school was very good to me as my mother had to work. Her name was Miss Tate. Other staff I remember were Miss Cramp and Mrs Cable in their flowery cotton overalls.

Life in the Junior school with the late Mr E R Corby (who wrote me a reference for my first teaching job at the late Rockingham Road Secondary School, Kettering) — I remember standing under the clock for being naughty and Mr Corby telling me off for hitting another pupil with a rounders bat. Singing lessons with Mrs Hircock, I was a sparrow because I couldn't sing! English lessons were fun, Mr Gardener read us Dickens from a big heavy book and if we moved he used the book on our heads. Miss Rees, Mr Smith, Miss Chastor and Miss Wildman, with her dark plaited hair round her ears. Miss Giles, who later became Mrs Smith and Miss Wager who later became Mrs Sharpe, who I actually taught with on the staff at Rockingham Road school. I remember being a court lady in one of the school productions, was it Hansel and Gretel? Lovely school dinners under the supervision of Miss Wright.

When at the Junior school I moved to Barton Seagrave where upon daily travelling on the school bus all round Burton Latimer. Running down the subway and playing kiss chase.

My school days were enjoyable, rounders and high jump on the field. Lovely stories and many friends. I was in the A class and I can remember clearly the rows of single desks in the hall for the dreaded 11+. I failed. But never mind, I must have had a good basic education at the old schools as on the 16 July 1989 I shall be celebrating thirty years in the teaching profession for this county.

Often I drive by the old schools they seem so small and yet as a child so large and some of the teachers a little frightening.

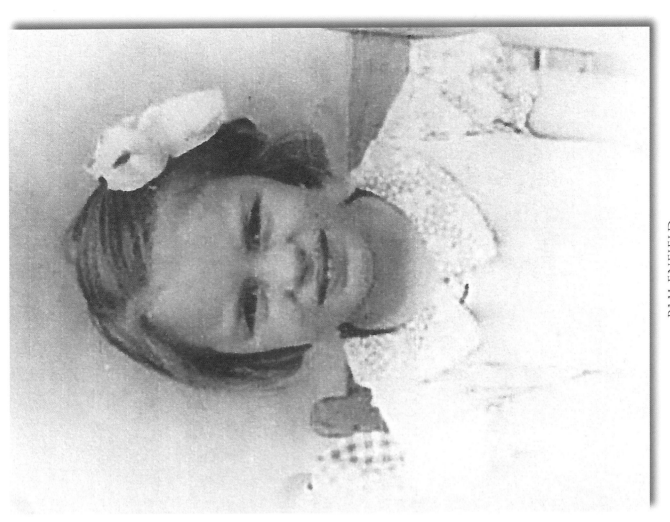

PAM ENFIELD

GILL ENFIELD

KETTERING URBAN DISTRICT EDUCATION COMMITTEE.

REGULATIONS RELATIVE TO CORPORAL PUNISHMENT.

The following is an Extract from the Committee's General Regulations :

The Head Teacher of each School has the right to administer Corporal Punishment, and Certificated Teachers, on obtaining their Parchment Certificate, may be empowered to administer Corporal Punishment to the Children in their own Classes, but this power shall not be exercised by any Certificated Teacher without the express authority of the Local Education Authority.

The Head Teacher is authorised to temporarily withdraw the power in the case of any Certificated Teacher administering excessive or improper punishment, pending the decision of the Authority.

Each Head Teacher, and each Certificated Teacher empowered as aforesaid, shall keep a Punishment Book, and shall immediately enter therein every case of punishment administered by him or her.

All Punishment Books to be submitted through the Head Teacher to the School Management Sub-Committee once a month, or oftener if required.

Under no circumstances shall any Teacher be permitted to strike a child on the head either with the hand or with any instrument whatsoever.

Punishment to be administered only by means of a cane, which will be supplied to the Teachers.

The date, the nature of offence, and the number of strokes administered as punishment to any child to be immediately recorded in the Punishment Book.

Any breach of the regulations of the Committee relating to Corporal Punishment will be severely dealt with.

HENRY GOTCH INFANTS
SCHOOL

PUNISHMENT BOOK.

Date of Punishment.	Name of Child Punished.	Nature of Offence.	No. of Strokes administered.
3. 10. 40	Capps, Reginald	Playing Truant	2 strokes
		PRODUCED AT COMMITTEE. 18 NOV 1940	
2. 4. 41.	Capps, Reginald	Playing Truant.	2 strokes.
		PRODUCED AT COMMITTEE. 21 ... 1941	
30. 6. 41.	Capps, Reginald	Playing Truant.	4 strokes
		PRODUCED...	
5. 9. 41	Capps, Reginald	Running away at playtime	4 strokes
		PRODUCED AT COMMITTEE. 17 NOV 1941	

Date of Punishment.	Name of Child Punished.	Nature of Offence.	No. of Strokes administered.
7. 7. 39	Max Cartony	Walking on the wall of the railway after being warned twice.	1 stroke
	KETTERING EDUCATION COMMITTEE / PRODUCED AT COMMITTEE 17 JUL 1939 / RECD 17 JUL 1939 ANSD — REF. N—		
17. 10. 39.	Eldon, John	Stone throwing against London children — dangerous being warned twice.	1 stroke.
	PRODUCED AT COMMITTEE. 20 NOV 1939		
12. 12. 39.	Argust, Patrick	Lit a stone in playground — hit Tanfield on head — made a small cut	2 strokes
4. 1. 40	Robert Giles, Terence Nicholls	Stone throwing — Terence Nicholls slightly cut on lip.	1 stroke each
	PRODUCED AT COMMITTEE. 15 JAN 1940		
13. 4. 40.	No Punishment		
	PRODUCED AT COMMITTEE. 15 APR 1940		
12. 7. 40	No Punishment		

(Top record)

Date of Punishment.	Name of Child Punished.	Nature of Offence.	No. of Strokes administered.
10.7.43	McMillan, Alan	Stone throwing	1 stroke
		PRODUCED AT COMMITTEE [stamp]	
21.7.43	Banfield, Frederick	throwing stone, breaking B. Norton's fences & cutting by	4 strokes
14.9.43	David Ashton	throwing stones & sticks and help after being warned	1 stroke
17.9.43	Ian Plowright	Playing near and telling which side of rings	1 stroke
21.9.43	David Keen, Alan McMillan, Terence Wakelin, Ian Plowright	Damaging tree	1 stroke
22.9.43	no punishments	Deliberately tearing reading book	1 stroke
		PRODUCED AT COMMITTEE 15 NOV 1943	
19.1.44	no punishments.		
		PRODUCED AT COMMITTEE [stamp]	

(Bottom record)

Date of Punishment.	Name of Child Punished.	Nature of Offence.	No. of Strokes administered.
17.4.42	No Punishments		
	PRODUCED AT COMMITTEE		
7.5.42	Clancy, Leonard	throwing a halfbrick at a little girl	1 stroke
7.6.42	John Tolley / John Horwell	Stealing canaries, chillos wild green leaf myrtle - after warned	2 strokes each
19.6.42	Leonard ...	do	1 stroke
21.6.42	Jack Roberts	breaking walls of ...	1 stroke
	PRODUCED AT COMMITTEE 20 ... 1942		
11.42	Ronald Diamond	getting into and milked cow using slang (numerous warnings given)	1 stroke
	PRODUCED AT COMMITTEE 16 NOV 1942		
17.4.43	...		
	PRODUCED AT COMMITTEE 12 APR 1943		

IMPORTANT WAR DATES

1939

Sep 1. Germany invaded Poland
Sep 3. Great Britain and France declared war on Germany; the B.E.F. began to leave for France
Dec 13. Battle of the River Plate

1940

Apr 9. Germany invaded Denmark and Norway
May 10. Germany invaded the Low Countries
June 3. Evacuation from Dunkirk completed
June 8. British troops evacuated from Norway
June 11. Italy declared war on Great Britain
June 22. France capitulated
June 29. Germans occupied the Channel Isles
Aug 8–Oct 31. German air offensive against Great Britain (Battle of Britain)
Oct 28. Italy invaded Greece
Nov 11–12. Successful attack on the Italian Fleet in Taranto Harbour.
Dec 9–11. Italian invasion of Egypt defeated at the battle of Sidi Barrani

1941

Mar 11. Lease-Lend Bill passed in U.S.A.
Mar 28. Battle of Cape Matapan
Apr 6. Germany invaded Greece
Apr 12–Dec 9. The Siege of Tobruk
May 20. Formal surrender of remnants of Italian Army in Abyssinia
May 20–31. Battle of Crete
May 27. German battleship *Bismarck* sunk
June 22. Germany invaded Russia
Aug 12. Terms of the Atlantic Charter agreed
Nov 18. British offensive launched in the Western Desert
Dec 7. Japanese attacked Pearl Harbour
Dec 8. Great Britain and United States of America declared war on Japan

1942

Feb 15. Fall of Singapore
Apr 16. George Cross awarded to Malta
Oct 23–Nov 4. German-Italian army defeated at El Alamein
Nov 8. British and American forces landed in North Africa

1943

Jan 31. The remnants of the 6th German Army surrendered at Stalingrad
May 1. Final victory over the U-Boats in the Atlantic
May 13. Axis forces in Tunisia surrendered
July 10. Allies invaded Sicily
Sep 3. Allies invaded Italy
Sep 8. Italy capitulated
Dec 26. *Scharnhorst* sunk off North Cape

1944

Jan 22. Allied troops landed at Anzio
June 4. Rome captured
June 6. Allies landed in Normandy
June 13. Flying-bomb (V.1) attack on Britain started
June 22. Defeat of Japanese invasion of India
Aug 25. Paris liberated
Sep 3. Brussels liberated
Sep 8. The first rocket-bomb (V.2) fell on England.
Sep 17–26. The Battle of Arnhem
Oct 20. The Americans re-landed in the Philippines

1945

Jan 17. Warsaw liberated
Mar 20. British recaptured Mandalay
Mar 23. British crossed the Rhine
Apr 25. Opening of Conference of United Nations at San Francisco
May 2. German forces in Italy surrendered
May 3. Rangoon recaptured
May 5. All the German forces in Holland, N.W. Germany and Denmark surrendered unconditionally
May 9. Unconditional surrender of Germany to the Allies ratified in Berlin
June 10. Australian troops landed in Borneo
Aug 6. First atomic bomb dropped on Hiroshima
Aug 8. Russia declared war on Japan
Aug 9. Second atomic bomb dropped on Nagasaki
Aug 14. The Emperor of Japan broadcast the unconditional surrender of his country
Sep 5. British forces re-entered Singapore

MY FAMILY'S WAR RECORD

8th June, 1946

To-day, as we celebrate victory, I send this personal message to you and all other boys and girls at school. For you have shared in the hardships and dangers of a total war and you have shared no less in the triumph of the Allied Nations.

I know you will always feel proud to belong to a country which was capable of such supreme effort; proud, too, of parents and elder brothers and sisters who by their courage, endurance and enterprise brought victory. May these qualities be yours as you grow up and join in the common effort to establish among the nations of the world unity and peace.

George R.I.

NURSERY SCHOOL LUNCHTIME, 1945

8th & 9th September 1945
The school is closed for
V.E. day. (End of WW2)

29th July 1946
First parents day is held.

TRIP TO LONDON ZOO 1946

Housewife

JANUARY 1946

NINEPENCE

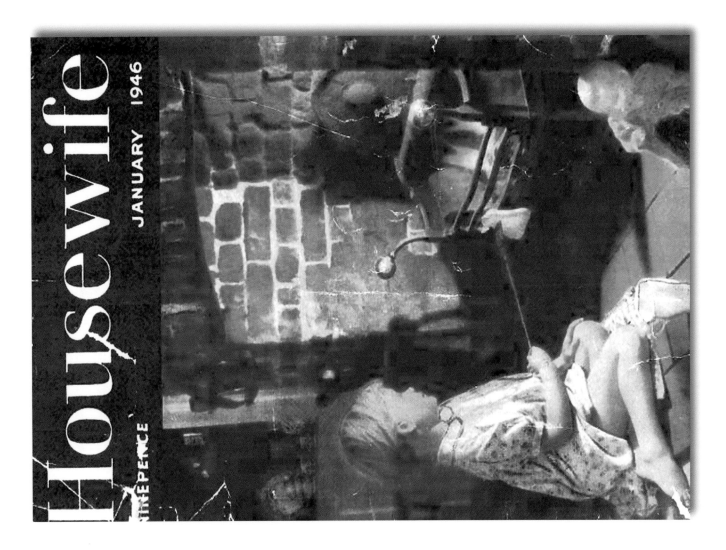

A MODEL SCHOOL IN THE COUNTRY

The entrance to the Infants' Department

ALTHOUGH so many of our country schools are a reproach to our whole educational system, some progressive and far-sighted communities have succeeded to a remarkable extent in providing excellent modern school buildings. One of these is the Henry Gotch Council School, at Kettering, in Northamptonshire. This school is of the one-storey type, built in such a way as to catch the maximum of sun, and all classes can move out into the open whenever the weather permits. But even in this modern school, each classroom holds as many as 48 pupils. An interesting feature is the subway built to avoid the danger of crossing the busy by-pass road on which the school stands. The school was opened in 1939 and cost £50,000. It accommodates 760 children, including 40 under-fives.

Every classroom has a southern aspect and the whole school moves out onto the veranda for open-air lessons

Six-year-olds have standard paint boxes with four colours which they use as they please. They are encouraged to give their imagination free play

Five-year-old Valerie and Janet enjoy their half pint of milk in the morning

Plenty of room for boys and girls to come out and play

Their midday meal at school

Handicraft class in progress

Three- and four-year-olds have an hour's nap after lunch.
Lying with heads in alternate order reduces the temptation to talk

Children do not need to cross the road to leave
school—a subway leads out of the grounds

The grounds extend over 18 acres

SUBWAY SUMMER, 1945

CHILDREN SEEING FRUIT FOR THE FIRST TIME. COMPLIMENTS OF THE CANADIAN
AIR FORCE, WHO WERE BILLOTED ON THE JUNIOR SCHOOL PLAYING FIELDS
DURING THE 2ND WORLD WAR 1947

MARRIAGE OF PRINCESS ELIZABETH TO DUKE OF EDINBURGH
JUNIOR SCHOOL, 1947

H.G. NURSERY 1948. PAT ANDREWS - JOHN SELLERS

WEDDING PHOTOS, PRINCESS ELIZABETH - DUKE OF EDINBURGH, 1948

JUNIOR SCHOOL STAFF, 1948

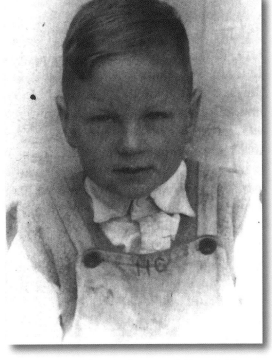

JOHN SELLERS, NURSERY 1948

3rd December 1948
Annual Prizegiving is
begun.

JOHN SELLERS, NURSERY 1948

JUNIOR SCHOOL ORCHESTRA, 1949

ANN BUSHNELL RECEIVES HER PRIZE.
PRIZE GIVING DAY, 1949

JOHN SELLERS AGED 5.
MISS CRAMPS CLASS, 1ST YEAR INFANTS 1949

I am a former pupil of the Infant, Junior and Senior schools. I grew up in Kettering in Piper's Hill Road, only a short walking distance from the three schools. I have many happy memories of all three schools.

My first year would have been 1949. I can still remember sitting on my mother's knee in the corridor outside the Headmaster's office, underneath the clock. It would have been either my first day at school or the day I was enrolled.

I remember the many years of walking along Windmill Avenue to school. Of walking down the subway. The rule of the schools was, for road safety, that if we lived on the opposite side of the road from the schools, we had to use the subway to gain entry to the schools. We were not to cross the road.

I can remember both the layouts of the Infant and Junior schools. Two sets of classrooms both sides of the quadrangle, hall at the top and cloakrooms at the bottom. We always started in the first year at the bottom left hand room of the school, graduating to the top rooms in ones final year. My final year in the Infants was spent in the top right hand classroom. My teacher was a Miss Hurcock. I also remember a Mr Furnell, who is now deceased. My first teacher in the Juniors was Mr Betts.

I can remember a few of my lessons - music in the hall playing instruments, dancing lessons. Playing with conkers, marbles, skipping ropes and whip and top in the playground. All the games would follow each year with the seasons.

The teacher in my last year in the Juniors was a lovely lady, Mrs. Evans. On my return visits home from Australia I've often met with Mrs. Evans. I also remember sitting for the 11+ examination in the school hall.

As you can see from my address I am now living in Australia. I've travelled many thousands of miles by sea and over land. I spent almost five years living in a trawling boat. It is a different way of life over here, and of course, the weather is wonderful.

I've had so many adventures here, far too many to mention. At the moment I am living in a small bush town half way up the western coast. The next town south is about 400 miles away, and the next one north is 300 miles. I could write a book of my adventures and travels in this country.

1950

TEACHERS

INFANTS

Miss Dorothy Cramp
Miss Mary Baum
Mrs Mabel Bates
Mrs Ethel Payne
Mrs Dorothy Thompson
Mrs Cable
Miss B Crawford
Miss Morris
Miss Thomas
Miss Beard
Miss M Osborne
Miss J Munday
Miss Abbott
Miss J M Wilson
Miss E Osborne
Mrs Moseley
Miss P M Mayes
Mrs Kendall
Miss Loake
Mrs Ellis
Mrs Glover
Mrs Whitney
Miss Wooster
Miss Warrington
Mrs Newell
Mrs Watson
Mrs Hughes
Miss Kane
Mrs Hooper
Mrs Butcher
Miss Smith
Mrs Nesbitt
Mrs Haigh
Mrs S Stokes
Mrs Shrigley-Hodgson
Mrs B Southwell
Mrs J Robinson
Miss A Brewin
Mrs W Cox
Miss K Guy
Miss M Senesse
Mrs J Partridge
Miss E Blakeley
Miss K Clarke

Miss Derrick
Miss Hinton
Mrs Fisher
Miss Joyce Earl
Miss L Kingsbury
Miss W M Hemmers
Miss Molly Cooke
Miss Cole
Miss Kay
Mrs Ball
Miss Sheila Bull
Miss Knight
Miss M A Stimson
Mrs M Goulding
Mrs R M Bell
Mrs B M Wills
Mrs Joyce Peasley
Miss J E Chapman
Miss A Lomas
Mrs Dunmore
Miss Ireton
Miss West
Mrs Munns
Miss Cawdell
Miss Thurland
Mrs Sliwinski
Mrs Smith
Mrs Johnson
Mrs Seddon
Mrs March
Miss Bottomley
Mrs Irene Bailey
Miss Lynne Maber
Mrs S Curtis/Oglethorpe
Mrs J Mossop
Mrs I Bithray
Mrs L Rose
Mr Blair
Mrs R Cuthbert
Mrs J Farthing
Miss A Remington
Miss A Wise
Miss R Walker

TEACHERS

JUNIORS

Mr E Corby

D A Rees

Mrs P Hircock

Mr J W Hannant

Miss E G Matthews

Mr D Wears

Mr G Freeman

Miss M C Morgan

Mr Burbridge

Mrs Lawson

Mrs Tuppen

Mr Stenning

Mrs A R Pedley

Mrs Calvert

Mrs P Shaw

Mrs P Warren

Mrs Danks

Mrs V Sawfoot

David Watt

Mrs Summerley

Mrs M McLennon

Mrs P Moseley

Mr J Miller

Mrs K Loveridge

Mrs J Tattersall

Mr J Toon

Mrs C Bell

Mr C Johnson

Miss G Ash (Lea)

Mrs A Fothergill

Miss J Briggs

Miss K McVeigh

Miss R Askew

Miss C Jenkins (Leeming)

Miss K Underwood (Freeman)

Mr R Hollwey

Miss Lilian Lenton

Miss Ruby Wileman

Miss Cunliffe

Miss N M Chaston

Mr L T Bird

Miss J Ireson (Fouhy)

Miss D Cramer

Mrs B Leach

Mrs Fisher

Mrs Hindle

Mrs Germain

Mr Buller

Mrs Higham

Mrs J Brownnutt

Mrs Parker

Mrs B A Bickerdike

Mrs Dawes

Muriel Wallis

Mrs E Dawson

Mr C Vose

Miss Ford

Miss J Monger

Mrs J Yeomans

Mrs P Price

Mrs J Speechley

Mr D Drew

Mrs Collis

Mrs K Wane

Miss K Cann (Greaves)

Mrs S Sherkle

Miss T Allsopp

Miss S Davies

Miss S Durham

Mrs T Bingham

Mrs A Walker

HEAD TEACHERS

INFANTS

Miss Jane Tate
Miss Millar
Mrs Florence Wyatt
Miss Dorothy Hall
Miss Ruby Senescall
Mrs L Y Townsend
Mrs Joyce Peasley
Mrs Deidre Sneath
Mrs Ann Asquith Ellis
Mrs Heather Donoyou

JUNIORS

Mr D P Birtwisle
Mr E Corby
Mr L C Sinclair
Mr John Wholley
Mr Ian Nelson
Mr Peter Mayles
Mr Mark Pevy

PRIMARY

Mrs Heather Donoyou
Mrs Elizabeth Smorfitt
Miss Anne O'Neill

DEPUTY HEAD TEACHERS / ACTING HEADTEACHERS

INFANTS

Miss O Davis
Miss Catherine White
Miss Dorothy Cramp (Fisher)
Mrs Cable
Miss Anne Spence
Mrs Margaret Hooper
Mrs Bithray
Mrs Georgina Dredge
Mrs Dawn Fernie

JUNIORS

Mr F Lilley
Mrs Rowles
Miss Amey
Mr M E Jones
Mr J Betts
Mr Denton
G l Evans
Mr Conrad Johnson
Mr Andrew Moorcroft
Mrs Diane Gee

PRIMARY

Pam Kirkland
Mr M Talbot
Miss J Hutchins

1950

"EARLY STARTER"

When I started at Henry Gotch Nursery I was 3 years old, and I had to stay all day. The reason for this was because my father had an accident at work and broke his leg, and was unable to work for a long time. As there were no benefits in those days, my mother had to go to work to keep us. I was the youngest of five children. The places at the Nursery were given to the most needy cases. There was a place going and it was between our family and another in St. Mary's Road. They gave it to us as Mum had no other source of income. With me at Nursery Mum was able to go to work until my father was well again.

I remember being very frightened about going to Nursery. At that young age being away from your mother all day seemed like forever. We all used to have little beds and our own covers. Every afternoon we were supposed to have a sleep. I can remember my cover even now, it was dark green with a milk bottle and a straw cut out of felt and sewn on to it. I can see it now, all these little beds put out all around the room.

Another day that comes to mind was making little yellow chicks. It must have been for Easter. The teacher made the chicks from cotton wool and card, she had a large bowl of yellow dye and dipped each chick into it.

My teacher in the Infant school was Miss Cook, I thought the world of her, as did my new friend Kay Haywood. We met that first day and became friends and have remained so ever since. The Headmistress at that time was Mrs Elliot.

My favourite lessons were P.E. and Music. P.E. was great fun with large mats so you didn't hurt yourself, and small square bean bags to throw. Then we had some new balls all assorted colours and they were plastic with holes in them. I seem to recall ropes that came out from the walls, although I'm not sure if this was in the Infant or Junior school. I enjoyed Music, we all had instruments at one time too. I dread to think what it sounded like. I ended up with a triangle because I was away when the instruments were allocated!

When I moved into the Juniors I recall we were just beginning to tell the time. I can remember more of the teachers in the Juniors, Mr Corby was Headmaster; Miss Wymant used to wear her hair plaited and wound round by her ears, a style that was called 'earphones'; Miss Metcalf, who married and became Mrs Fitton while I was in her class; Mrs Hircock, who had taught my two brothers and two sisters before me, always ended the lessons reading us a story. I really enjoyed that, one in particular about a kingfisher springs to mind. My final teacher was Miss Worth, who seemed very young and very nice. I often see her locally, I believe her name is Mrs Watson now.

We used to have an assembly every morning and sing hymns and say prayers, I loved singing and was in the choir. Whenever I hear hymns it always reminds me of school assemblies. We used to have concerts at Easter and Christmas and it was thought very exciting if we had a concert in the evening. The Sports Days were also very enjoyable, even though I very rarely won anything. I think I once came third in an egg and spoon race and had a ribbon pinned on my blouse and it was great to sit with your class cheering on your friends.

Other teachers I can remember were Mrs. Evans, Mr Smith, who later taught at Park Road School and Mr Furnell. Another fond memory was morning break and your daily bottle of milk with a straw. I loved it. If anyone didn't want theirs I can remember one boy, Richard Allely, would always be able to drink a second bottle.

When I was in the Junior school the punishment for misbehaving was to be sent downstairs "under the clock". This was a clock in the corridor just outside the Headmaster's door. If you were really badly behaved the Headmaster would give you the slipper or the cane. I can honestly say fear of this made me behave, and thankfully, I was never sent "under the clock".

Mrs Jacqueline Paling (nee Mayers)

JUNIOR SCHOOL STAFF, CIRCA 1952

CHOIR CELEBRATE JUNIOR SCHOOL'S
NEW POND, CIRCA 1952

JUNIOR SCHOOL
MORRIS DANCING TEAM, 1952

15th February 1952
The school listens to the
radio broadcast the
funeral of King George 6th

JUNIOR SCHOOL NATIVITY PLAY, 1952

JUNIOR MORRIS DANCING TEAM, 1952

JUNIOR SCHOOL PRIZE GIVING, 1953

Northamptonshire Education Committee.

KETTERING

Henry Gotch County Primary School

(JUNIOR DEPT.)

REPORT.

July 1953.

Name. Barry Basford   Class. 8

Pos. in Age Group ...... 43 ...out of...... 92

Pos. in Class.......... 6 ...... out of........ 39

Arithmetic	58·5	Spelling	55·5
English	47	Composition	70
Reading	67·5	General	50
Writing	50	Handwork and Art	50

NOTE. All these marks are 'Standardised,' i.e the range of marks in every subject is the same with a top mark of about 73 and a bottom mark of 27. 50 is the average.

All children of the same age do the same tests in Arithmetic, Reading, English and Writing in order to ascertain the child's position in the Age Group.

Attendance V. Good.   Behaviour. Good.

General Remarks. A painstaking boy who has reached a high position in the class through real hard work.

Class Teacher. J.R. Betts

Headmaster.

Parent's Signature

TYPICAL JUNIOR SCHOOL REPORT, 1950'S

JUNIOR SCHOOL PRIZE GIVING, 1953

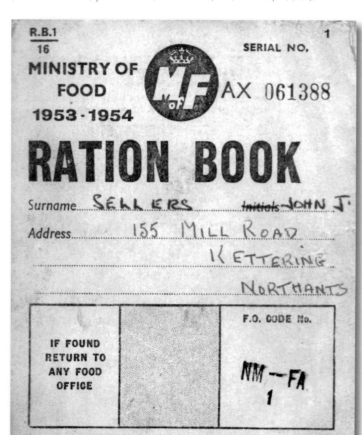

R.B.1		1
16		SERIAL NO.

MINISTRY OF FOOD

1953-1954

AX 061388

RATION BOOK

Surname SELLERS   Initials JOHN J.

Address 155 MILL ROAD

KETTERING

NORTHANTS

F.O. CODE No.

IF FOUND RETURN TO ANY FOOD OFFICE

NM – FA 1

JOHN SELLERS' RATION BOOK

NEW SCHOOL OPENED 1953
COST £143,107, 208 PUPILS

11th November 1953
The school is broken into.
£3 worth of damage is done.

JUNIOR SCHOOL PRIZE GIVING, 1953

HENRY GOTCH PRIZE GIVING, 1953

MISS PAYNE'S CLASS, 1954

FORM 1B MRS CLARKE'S CLASS

FORM IV MR JOHNSON'S CLASS

THE WALLER FAMILY, STAUNCH SUPPORTERS
AND PUPILS OF HENRY GOTCH JUNIOR SCHOOL

VIEW OF SCHOOL FROM RIVER ISE

PLAYING FIELDS BEFORE THE
BULLDOZERS MOVED IN

DEEBLE ROAD, SUMMER OF 1954

FORM III MR DAVIS'S CLASS

STAFF 1954

Left to Right: Back row – Mr Dollery, Mr Davis, Mr Plews, Mr Johnson, Mr Morley.
Front Row – Mrs Clarke, Mr Lewin, Mrs Brownlee, Miss Shorter.

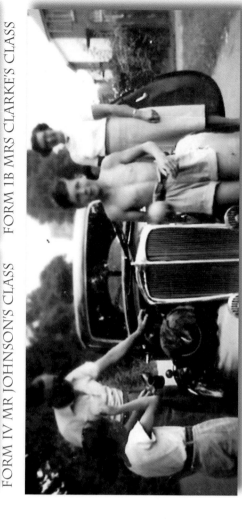

JUNIOR SCHOOL PTA DANCE, 1954

MR WALLER'S STALL, JUNIOR SCHOOL FETE, 1954

MRS EVANS CLASS, JUNIORS 1955

MRS EVANS CLASS, JUNIORS 1955

"BEAUTY & THE BEAST" –
JUNIOR SCHOOL PLAY, 1955

UNDISPUTED JUNIOR SCHOOL SACK RACE CHAMPION - GODFREY MORRIS
Left to Right: Back row - Humphrey, Judy Clipstone. Front row - Godfrey Morris, Jeff Waller, Richard Curtis, Patrick Waller

JUNIOR SCHOOL SACK RACE, 1955
Left to Right: Tommy Welsh, Robert Apel, Philip Ince, Jeff Waller

MR FURNELL'S CLASS, CIRCA 1955

In September 1955, 42 nervous youngsters entered form 1A in Henry Gotch Secondary Modern School. Secondary Modern pupils in 1955 were fondly referred to as "Factory Fodder".

6 of class 1A would become millionaires, many would run highly successful businesses, others would rise to high ranks in the police force and army etc. Many would make important contributions to their local communities!

JUNIOR SCHOOL MAGAZINE 1955

MR WATTS' CLASS 1C, 1955

MRS BROWNLEE'S FORM IIA, 1955

MR MARTIN'S FORM III, 1955

SCHOOL PLAY, 1955

JENNIFER DADD AS
THE COUNTESS DE MONTAIGNE

PEASANT DANCERS

SENIOR SCHOOL STAFF, 1955

MR BRIGGS' CLASS, 1955

MISS WHITE CLASS 1B, 1955

SCHOOL FETE, 1955

SCHOOL FOREIGN HOLIDAY, 1955

MISS COOKE'S INFANT CLASS, 1955-6. ENJOYING A NATURE WALK

Teacher - Margaret Watson

I began my teaching career at Henry Gotch Junior School in the fifties and I
have fond memories of the staff and children. Mr Eric Corby was the headmaster
at the time and the school boasted a population of about 420 pupils.

One day (in 1956/7 I think) a new admission made my second year 'A' class
complement rise to 49! I well recall my colleague George Furnell quietly telling
me that if just one more pupil signed in, the class would reach the magic number
of 50, and then I would qualify for a terrific rise in salary! As a very raw
recruit I really believed him, and indeed, I remember feeling considerable
disappointment when one 'inmate' had the audacity to move house. With only 48
children the chance to make my fortune was slipping away.

MISS EVANS' JUNIORS CLASS, CIRCA 1956

MR SMITH'S CLASS, 1956

JUNIOR SCHOOL NATIVITY PLAY, 1956

'THE SARACENS HEAD', SENIOR SCHOOL PLAY 1956

GARDENING, 1956

SENIOR SCHOOL CHOIR, 1956

SENIOR SCHOOL STAFF, 1956

THE KING'S ENGLISH
DRAMA FESTIVAL, 1956

'THE SARACENS HEAD', SENIOR SCHOOL PLAY, 1956

NEW TENNIS COURTS, 1956

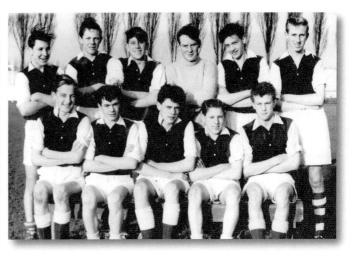

SENIOR U 15 SOCCER TEAM, 1956-57

SCHOOL SPORTS, 1956

U 13 SOCCER TEAM, 1956-57

SCHOOL SPORTS DAY, AVONDALE PLAYING FIELD, 1956

THE SCHOOL PLAY, 1956

"Paint and Powder"

Shortly before half term, those who were keen to have a part in the Christmas play, attended an audition held in the Art room. We read different speeches from the script and as soon as the parts were cast, we began to copy our lines. Many rehearsals followed this, and those who had leading parts found we were needed quite often as the time of the play drew near. In fact, we often had to try to be in two places at once!

All the cast were now busy collecting their costumes together and having dress-parades under the expert eye of Miss Sowerby. At last everything was ready; the scenery in position and the car in the wings, (this later caused much fun, running over people's toes and some of the properties).

Eventually the first night came: the leading characters, Roger Dodson, Tommy Welsh, Yvonne Taylor, Roger Knight and I, were all made up and waiting nervously for our cues. As the play carried on, the crew of the car, who were now beginning to get used to the pulling and dragging, were forgetting their nervousness and really lost themselves in the story, which was about a car entered in the " Monte Carlo Rally " without the driver knowing.

Sometimes during the performances, things did not go quite according to plan, but these incidents are quite amusing to look back on. Our audiences seemed to appreciate our efforts, thus making the hours of rehearsal time seem well spent. By the way, does it ever snow when the sun is shining anywhere else?

CHRISTINE FENNELL.

Scenery Painting

Four weeks before our play, " The Monte Carlo Rally " three boys from 4A, Roger Dodson, Anthony Crick, and myself were chosen to paint the backcloths for the play. We were later joined by Melvin Stirmey and Neil Pyburn.

Our first job was to design the main scenes, then to work out a colour scheme, limiting ourselves to certain colours at first. As soon as we had designed the first scenes and mixed the colours required, we brought out the old backcloths used in our previous production, " Appointment with the Guillotine." On these we chalked the scenes. There were six scenes in the play, five of which had painted backcloths. We then laid out the backcloths in the foyer, this being the only available space.

The first scene we painted showed a French cafe at Mâcon. The second was an Alpine scene, probably our most colourful. Then

16

came the " Casino Grand " in Monte Carlo, which was designed by Mr. Dollery. The fourth scene was a Frontier Post on the edge of the " Iron Curtain." Finally we painted the departure scene, in the Garden of Joseph Jowett's home.

On the nights of the play we were told that the scenery was quite effective especially under stage lighting, so we felt our backaches had been worth while !

JOHN COX

FACTS ON THE PLAY :—3 Full Houses . . . a £5 Car . . . Yodelling and Alpine Dances . . . Cossack dancing and gymnastics, with fleas and beards . . . A Dream Scene—of " One Night in Paris " . . . A Snowstorm in the Alps . . . Newspaper properties supplied by the " Evening Telegraph " . . . " Get out and Get Under " . . . " We're Riding Along on the Crest of a Wave " . . . A Carnival, a Casino and a Band . . . and ours was the only " Monte Carlo Rally " held anywhere this winter—petrol rationing did not prevent ours from being held.

Ode To Homework

This is no joy
For a healthy boy
It's more like crime
To write in ryhme.
It's not quite right
On this perfect night
To sit at a table
And not be able
A poem to write
(Not being so bright).
My idea of joy
For a healthy boy
Is to be out and away
At game and at play.

P. DRING.

ALL THE FUN OF THE FAIR !

Our School Fete was to be held on Saturday, June 9th 1956, on the School terraces according to the programme ! Unfortunately the weather was undecided whether to favour us or flood us out. After this set-back we thought we had better hold it inside the school, so all the stalls were hurriedly taken down and pushed back inside, to be set up again in the Hall and Cloakrooms. Many pupils and Parents' Association members were erecting and decorating the stalls and school terraces. Two of our form mates were checking all the entries for the cake competition. Entries came in in great numbers, ranging from dark brown ones to golden brown ones and in all shapes and sizes. By the end of the morning they were ready for judging by a local catering expert.

17

SCHOOL MAGAZINE, 1957

3RD YEAR JUNIORS, 1957

HENRY GOTCH JUNIORS, MRS HIRCOCKS CLASS, 1956-57

3RD YEAR JUNIORS, 1957

HENRY GOTCH JUNIORS, MR FURNELLS CLASS, 1956-57

LETTERS TO THE EDITOR

Dear Sir,

Are teenagers' parents being fair to look down upon the ever-popular Rock 'n' Roll? There isn't much difference between that and the " Charleston." which was so popular long ago. This form of music is energetic and lively, and it is quite obvious that thousands of youngsters show their appreciation by buying records. In several years' time, another craze will become popular, and Rock 'n' Roll will be looked upon as out-of-date. Of course many of today's so-called Teddy-boys took advantage of Rock 'n' Roll, to start rioting, and then this music was blamed for the damages, and the anti-Rock 'n' Rollers were only too pleased to blame the new craze. I hope that many people who despise this music will soon realise that it is a form of enjoyment, not just an opportunity to show-off or riot.

Yours sincerely,
H.J.

Dear Sir,

What is your opinion of Rock 'n' Roll? I think it is very amusing to watch other teenagers using up their surplus energy, crazily rocking over the floor, thinking they are doing the supposed dance correctly. But this is not for me!

Although there is a tremendous noise at sessions where these dances are performed, I suppose it is better than having the noisy and riotous gangs of youths in the street.

Yours sincerely,
A.C.

Dear Sir,

As this will be the last chance I will get, I would like to thank everyone concerned for their very fine efforts to raise money for our school's new swimming pool.

I would especially like to congratulate the Parents' Association on the magnificent work they are doing by organizing such events as Whist Drives, Dances and Raffles. If they continue at the present rate there will soon be enough money to pay for it.

I think that the idea of a swimming pool is very good, because it will give more people a chance to be taught how to swim.

Yours sincerely,
NEIL PYBURN.

Dear Sir,

I think the idea of having a swimming pool in a school's grounds is not a good one.

During the summer months, the dogs which roam around the school's grounds, will be playing in the pool, taking in with them, mud and dirt.

If it is not separated from the other surrounding areas, children from the school, or from other schools may be tempted to play around it, and accidents may occur.

Yours faithfully,
M.S.

Editor—We hope to prevent the above hazards.

Dear Sir,

I think that taking parties of children on foreign holidays is a very good idea. Many of the children who go on these holidays, will perhaps never get another chance to go abroad.

I myself went on the foreign holiday last year and thoroughly enjoyed the experience. I think that any children who have a chance like this, should take it if they possibly can.

Yours sincerely,
V.W.

Dear Sir,

In my opinion, there should be more stadiums or tracks built to give young athletes the opportunity to train. I know of a young man, not yet twenty, who is very good at putting the shot.

In his day's work, he has to carry long heavy bars, and this no doubt helps him very much to build up powerful muscles. In addition to this, he trains during his breaks and dinner hour, lifting pairs of truck wheels, while his workmates look on.

At night he trains with a proper shot, and he also runs over slag heaps to increase his stamina. He is only one of the many young but promising athletes who live too far from a track to train properly under skilled coaches. I think if such people were given the proper facilities and training, Britain would win more gold medals in the Olympic Games.

Yours faithfully,
ALAN STAPLETON.

SCHOOL MAGAZINE, 1957

SUMMARY OF EMPLOYMENT ENTERED BY SCHOOL LEAVERS
DECEMBER, 1953, TO DECEMBER, 1956, (4 YEARS).

BOYS
Engineering (4 Motor, 4 General 4 Pattern making, 2 cycle repairs)	14
Electricians	6
Boot and Shoe Industry	9
Building Trades (Carpentry, Building, Plumbing Decorating)	14
British Railways	9
Farming	9
Shop Assistants	6
General Labouring, etc. and Factory Work	8
Office Workers and Executive Trainees	7
Further Education	8
	90

GIRLS.
Boot and Shoe Industry	21
Clothing Industry	13
Office Work	12
Shop Assistants	10
Weetabix	5
Further Education	1
Left the District	3
	65

THE PARENTS' ASSOCIATION

Chairman: Mr. Dennis Corby, 4 Mill Dale Road, Kettering.
Joint Vice-Chairmen:
Mr. E. Maxey, 171 Stamford Road, Kettering.
Mr. E. Plews, 4 Hood Walk, Kettering.
Secretary: Mrs. K. Humfrey, 7 Larch Road, Kettering.
Treasurer: Mr. F. F. Ashwell, 12 Meadway Close, Kettering.
Catering Secretary: Mrs. Crick, 35 West Avenue, Burton Latimer.

To the Editor,
School Magazine   March 1957.
Dear Sir,

Before presenting a brief resumé of some of the Parents' Association's activities for the past year, I must in truly British fashion comment on the beautiful early Spring weather we are enjoying at the end of an exceptionally mild winter.

In the Spring of last year our menfolk turned out in splendid numbers and varied costumes, to play the school at football. We were defeated then, and again in the Summer at Cricket, to the delight of the school, but on both occasions onlookers and players alike spent very enjoyable evenings. (Repercussions next day on some of the parent-players need not be mentioned!) Undaunted and undismayed, we shall try hard to retrieve our honour on both fields this year.

In September last, at school morning assembly, members of the committee (there was not room for many), were present when

Mr. Harold Taylor, as Chairman of the Governors, accepted the Inter-House Honours Board as a gift from the Parents' Association to the school. In this excellent and attractive work, so ably executed by Mr. Morley, the Handicrafts master of the school, we can feel proud to have presented something of permanent value to the school's life.

Another successful Dutch Auction was also held in September, 1956, thanks to many gifts of clothing, etc., by parents and friends. We hope to repeat this event in September, 1957, so please put on one side, any articles you have to spare, for collection in the first week of the September term.

We again gave four prizes for public spirit, two for seniors and two for juniors, which were presented at the school Speech Day. We also gave school parties to the pupils in February this year, one for juniors, and one for seniors on St. Valentine's Day, February 14th. If fun and noise and the shouts for " more " are anything to go by, a good time was enjoyed by all. Notable to me was the happy, carefree romp of the juniors, compared with the more sedate behaviour of the seniors, especially with dancing, except of course during " Rock and Roll " Sessions.

Committee members have also helped at several school functions, concerts, drama festival, etc. We have enjoyed a talk with films, by Mr. Roger Banks on his explorations in Antarctica. Likewise, Mr. Valvona, the County Road Safety Officer, gave us a varied film programme; and last October, a Male-Voice Choir, from the American Air-base at Molesworth, gave us an impressive concert.

Our Socials and Whist-Drives continue merrily as a regular feature of our programme. A new innovation this year was a Harvest Festival with Supper and Dance, which, like the Annual Dinner Dance was among the highlights of the year's social activities.

Last June, we raised over £200 at a very successful Garden Fete. It was successful in spirit, from the opening ceremony by Jack Gardner in a splendid message to youth, and also successful in the excellent financial result, achieved only by the hard work of the many helpers, parents and friends, too numerous to mention or thank individually. This success has led us to be ambitious enough to try to provide a swimming pool for the school with the £200 as a financial basis for the scheme. Having obtained the necessary permission from the County Council and the Ministry of Education, we are now working on ideas obtained from similar projects in other parts of the country, in order to amalgamate the best from each into our own bath, to prepare a detailed plan of construction for the approval of the County Architect. We hope that much of the labour will be voluntary and soon the call will be going out for helpers, skilled and unskilled (again in varied costumes and with various

HENRY GOTCH JUNIORS, CIRCA 1956–57

SENIOR SPORTS RECORD BREAKERS, 1957

SENIORS SCHOOL PLAY, MONTE CARLO RALLY, 1957

LEFT: THE SCHOOL'S
ATHLETICS TEAMS
FOR THE DISTRICT
SPORTS IN JUNE,
1957

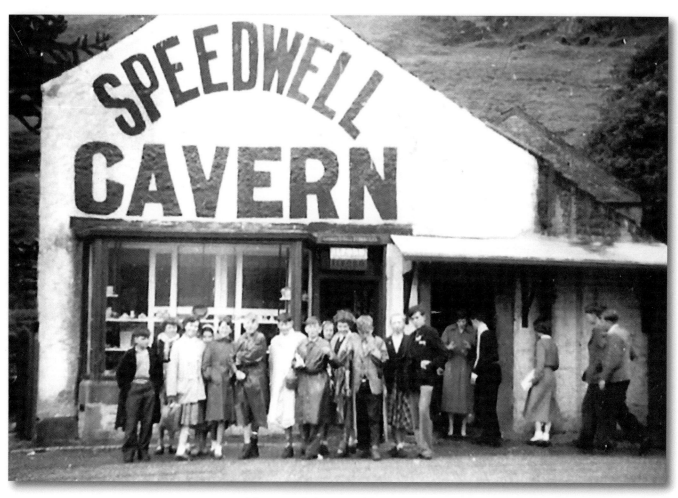

SENIOR SCHOOL TRIP, 1957

WORK STARTS ON THE SWIMMING POOL, SEPTEMBER 1957

MR LAWRENCE'S CLASS, JUNIOR SCHOOL, CIRCA 1958

MRS WILDMAN'S CLASS, CIRCA 1957-58

TOP YEAR JUNIORS, 1958

MR LAWRENCE'S CLASS, 1957-58

MRS EVAN'S CLASS, 1958
FEATURING PENNY, THE CARETAKER'S DOG

NEW CHERRY-RED UNIFORM INTRODUCED. MODELLED BY DEBORAH PEACOCK,
WITH LINDSEY JENKIN AND HER BROTHER NEIL, 1957-58

MRS WILDMAN'S CLASS, 1957-58

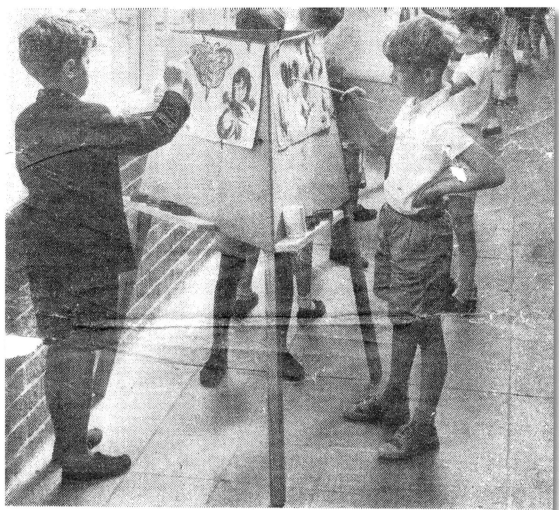

Bright ideas help Henry Gotch pupils improve their art

NO more jolted elbows, aching wrists and crabbed styles for these budding artists at Henry Gotch Junior School, Kettering, as they use their new easels in the school corridor instead of sitting hunched over their desks.

\SS 3 at the Henry Gotch Junior School, Ket-
.ring, had to stand in the corridor yesterday.
'+ they were not in disgrace . . . just using their
' studio-corridor for an art lesson.

leave plenty of room for teacher to move among the youngsters.

BIG CLASSES

The corridor, with its glass roof and plenty of windows, was just the answer.

But classes at the school are big—there are 45 budding artists in Class 3—and he was faced with the problem of getting enough easels into the comparatively restricted space.

Once again Mr. Corby came up with an original solution —a three-sided easel.

He designed the new piece of equipment and had about 16 made. Now the 40-plus classes can paint in comfort —ranged along the corridor in groups of three.

EXPRESSIVE

Already there are signs of improvement in the children's

OPENING OF THE SWIMMING POOL, JULY 4TH 1958

VIEW OF SWIMMING POOL

SCHOOL REPORT

FOR _Summer_ TERM, 195 8:

NAME _Barry Basford_   FORM _2B_

Age _13_ years _5_ months   Average Age of Form _13 5/12_   Number in Form _35_   Position in Form _#6_

Subject	% of Marks	Position	Remarks	Teacher
English :-				
Writing			Barry gets on with the job and eventually	
Reading	70		produces satisfactory results, but I would	
Spelling	62	25	like to see quicker thinking and more drive	C.J.M.
Composition	B		applied to written work. Spelling is still	
Literature	72	12 ·	rather shaky, and could be improved	
1	67½	21	by more reading.	
Mathematics	50	15	Steady in mechanical work.	P.P.
	44	14	Thoughtful, though slow, in problems	
Scripture	58	6 ·	Good work.	
History	51	13	Has shown interest & plodded steadily on, always doing his best.	
Art	77	2 ·	Always does his best.	
Crafts Social Studies	71	10 ·		
Geography	51	15 ·	Fairly good. Shows much interest.	
Science	58	9 ·	Good. Usually tries hard	
Needlework / Gardening				
Technical Drawing	72	5 ·	Has knowledge and ability and works well.	
Woodwork	84	1	A most promising craftsman.	
Metalwork	60	14 =	Quite good.	H.d.S.
Domestic Science				
Music	96	2	Always works well in Form & Violin Class	B
P.E. and Games			Not built to be a great gymnast, but performs creditably & shows a good attitude to the subject	

ATTENDANCE. _361_ out of _379_ good.

CONDUCT _Very good - a most cheerful and pleasant disposition, coupled with a willingness to help. His out-of-class help is greatly appreciated_

PROGRESS _has been maintained._

_____ J R Rowsby _____ Form Teacher.

Good in all ways — he shows

TYPICAL SENIOR SCHOOL REPORT, 1958

IN RETIREMENT

THE PONY CLUB

The Pony Club is a Youth Organisation for those interested in ponies and riding. It is represented in many countries and has a membership exceeding thirty thousand.

Carolyn Hanger.

"PRETTY BOY"

TEDDY BOYS AND GIRLS

CATS

A kitten is a very pretty plaything but like any other animal it has to be fed and looked after. Choose a kitten between nine and twelve weeks old.

HORSE RIDING

If you wish to learn to ride a horse, the first step you would take, would be to buy slacks or jodhpurs.

Joan Roberts.

SCHOOL SPORTS, 1957

J. Ridout.

SCHOOL UNIFORM

Dear Sir,

Yours faithfully,
C. W. Wickett (Miss).

HOMEWORK

Dear Sir,

Yours faithfully,
N. Perkins (Miss)

LITTER

Dear Sir,

Ian Willis

CRICKET (1957 SEASON)

The Athletics Champions were:

Senior Girls — June Wright and Ann Toseland
Boys — Peter Dring
Middle Girls — Pat Baker
Boys — John Yates
Junior Girls — Kay Taylor
Boys — Gordon Toseland

ROY SHRUBSALL

The School was shocked and grieved to hear of Roy's death in February of this year.

ALTHORP HOUSE NOTES

ARMY CADETS

M. A. Kyle.

"NEWSPAPERING"

Paul Hobbs.

"SPUTNIKS, SATELLITES AND ALL THAT."

John Mumbray.

NURSERY & INFANT SCHOOL STAFF, 1959

Left to Right: Back row - Mrs Cosby, Mrs Cable, Mrs Bell, Miss Bushnell, Mrs Bolton, Miss Loake

Front row - Miss Cole, Miss Hall (Head), Miss Cramp

JUNIORS, CIRCA 1958

JUNIORS, CIRCA 1959

MISS BUSHNELL'S CLASS, CIRCA 1959

MISS BUSHNELL'S NURSERY CLASS, 1959

MISS BUSHNELL'S INFANT CLASS, 1959

MR LAWRENCE'S CLASS, CIRCA 1959

1951 to 1955	Nursery		Miss Knight
			Miss Wilson
	Infants	Head	Mrs Ullyat
			Mrs Cable
			Miss Molly Cooke
			Miss Cramp
			Mrs Cable
			Mrs Stimpson
	Junior	Head	Mr Eric R Corby
			Mrs Lee Evans
			Mr George Furnell "Fuzzy"
			Mrs Phyllis Hircock
			Miss Payne
			Miss Ruby Willeman
	Secondary	Head	Mr Lewen
		Deputy	Miss Barr
		Music	Mr Briggs "Baldy"
			Mr Coleman
			Miss Hetherington
			Mr Johnson
			Mr Neil
			Mr Pridmore
			Mr Rosebury
			Mr Smith
			Miss Spence
1956 to 1960 As above plus:			
	Junior		Mr Drake
			Mr Lawrence
			Miss Marlow
			Mrs Mary Rowles
			Miss Margaret Worth (Mrs Watson)

Pupil - Lesley Lawman

I attended Henry Gotch Junior School at the end of the 1950's. The Headmaster was Mr Corby and my teacher was Miss Worth, who married and later became Mrs Watson.

There were 41 pupils in the class and we used to sit in pairs. The desks were quite heavy and had ink wells in the corner. Sometimes you would be chosen to be 'milk monitor'. This meant you would give the milk out to the rest of the class and then be responsible for putting the bottles back in the crates, when everyone was finished. Another job was quadrangle duty, this involved making sure nobody was playing in the quadrangle area and also feeding the fish in the fishpond, which was in the corner.

When it came to playtime, marbles were played also skipping and a game called five stones. These were five square wooden shaped objects which you put in the palm of your hand and then caught them on the other side of your hand. There were various games you did with these. There were also apparatus on the playing fields which you could play on.

1959

SCHOOL TRIP, 1959-60
Anita Clipstone, Richard Barratt, Lindsey Jenkins

SCHOOL TRIP, 1959-60
Teacher Mary Rowles. Smiling inside coach is Barry Jones, school centre forward.

JUNIORS CHRISTMAS NATIVITY PLAY, 1959

SENIOR FOOTBALL TEAM, 1959

"KING AND I" SENIOR SCHOOL PLAY, 1959

SENIOR SCHOOL
"SPORTSMAN OF THE YEAR"
KENNY PARFITT
IN TYPICAL POSE

HENRY GOTCH SECONDARY SCHOOL

SCHOOL MAGAZINE

No 5

JULY 1959

SCHOOL MAGAZINE COVER, 1959

BOB APEL, HENRY GOTCH'S MOST SUCCESSFUL SPORTSMAN

the Y.H.A., and was pleased to hear of this school's previous trips by cycle and on foot using this Association. Swimming is one of his favourite sports, so his aim is to see a school of almost all swimmers.

Like Mr. Lewin, Mr. Brittle is the father of a boy and a girl and his family are now living in Barton Seagrave. *Editor.*

ALTHORP HOUSE NOTES

During the school year 1957/58 we managed to add two shields to the Honours Board, the girls having won the tennis and the combined efforts of girls and boys giving us first place in the Athletics Competition. This year's successes so far are in the Cross Country and Hockey Competitions. Our Netball Team came third and the Football Team fourth. At the end of last Autumn term Mr. Johnson, our founder head of house, got a transfer (at no fee at all!) and now plays for a Market Harborough school. Mr. Gregg, who replaced Mr. Johnson, is our new " chief " and we extend a warm welcome to him; also to Mr. Gray, who joined us last September. We shall be sorry to lose Miss Head at the end of this term.

Easter saw the departure from us of Janice Smith, our regular reader at Althorp services, and Sam Payne, both House Captains, also Christine Ludlow, Althorp pianist and Vice Captain. We thank them for their services to the house. Our present Captains are Pamela Brice and Murray Berwick. We look forward to more successes in the athletic events of this term. J.R.R.

DRAYTON HOUSE NOTES

On the whole, we have had quite a succesful year, although many results were seconds and thirds rather than firsts.

In the Festival last year, Drayton almost won, being narrowly beaten by Kirby. Our boys did well in cricket too.

The Autumn term brought another second place. This time in the Merit Mark Competition. It was also marked by the loss at Christmas of our only lady member of staff, Miss Spencer, who left to take up another post at Sheffield.

Spring term, 1959, was brightened by the victory of our Netball team. Thanks to some good team work, and accurate shooting by Ellen Toseland, the sernior team won the event. This team was captained by Pat Andrews, and our juniors who played quite well though with slightly less success, had Marie Oram as Captain. Our footballers played some good games, giving us another second place on this competition.

During the spring term we also received a second place in the Merit Mark Competition.

At present, we are making plans for the last Inter-House events this school year, and we hope that our present House Captains Carol Scott and Robert Apel, will have the satisfaction of seeing us win the athletics before they leave us. MAVIS RIPPIN

6

KIRBY HOUSE NOTES

This last year seems to have been one of individual achievements for Kirby House members, rather than one of success for the whole house. Although at last Speech Night we received the Peck Cup, we cannot claim any real honours this school year, except for good performances by our Junior Netball Team, and our Senior Football Team. Perhaps one year we may have a team of cross-country runners instead of one junior winner (P. Oram) and a number of keen but unsuccessful triers. Our Senior Netball Team could have won the competition if they had not been handicapped by missing players. We must congratulate Frances Atterbury on her successes this last year. In School, District, and one friendly sports meeting, she has done very well, and her efforts in the Junior Netball Team too, were very useful.

Merit marks do not seem to have come our way so much this year. Our present juniors must try harder in this direction before we can expect any improvement.

We have had several changes of House Captains since the last magazine. Those at present serving are Leslie Betts and John Sellers, assisted by Christine Payne and Michael Rogers. We are pleased to have had additions to the members of staff in Kirby House, Mr. C. Smith and Mrs. Watson now being associated with our efforts A.G.M.

LILFORD HOUSE NOTES

Although we did quite well in last year's Peck Cup competition, winning the Football, P.E. and Swimming competitions, we finished 4th when the final positions were announced; merit marks having been the cause of our downfall; too few being gained and too many being lost.

We congratulate all who worked to give us our sports successes and those who gained our merit marks.

This year we have again won the Football Shield which we seem determined to make our own property and in merit marks we have made a good beginning by leading for two terms; let us hope we can keep this position for the year.

We welcome all newcomers to the house and it seems as if the " new blood " has inspired some of the older members to greater effort.

Unfortunately we carry our full share of " slackers " or as Mr. Marley used to call them " drones " who do very little towards our successes, but perhaps we can hope that our " transfusion " will prove a shot in the arm for Lilford House.

Our house captains are Susan Wallis and Roger Whitmee. Susan has been captain for over a year and has worked very hard for the house in many ways. Roger has only recently been appointed and it is to be hoped that both get the full support of the house.

EXAMINATIONS MAY BE DULL—
But some answers are rather amusing.
A camel carries its babies in its pocket.
A camel is useful because it will pull your trailer.

7

boys on a visit to the Stewart and Lloyd's works at Corby, and from what we have heard, they had a very enjoyable day.

At the end of July we shall be leaving and going off to take our places in the world of trade and industry.

I think on the whole we are a very intelligent and well-behaved form! ! ! S. WALLIS, P. BRICE, D. WHITNEY

4C FORM NOTES

In our form there are 26 pupils, 8 of these are very used to travelling on the school buses to and from Burton Latimer. Our form teacher is Mr. Gray who came at the beginning of the school year in September, 1958. Our form-room is in the centre wing and conveniently situated at the end of the corridor. Five of us are prefects and monitors including myself. After Easter we were joined with old 4D due to the small numbers in our class. Three boys and one girl took part in the Town Sports and we enjoyed ourselves very much. We are all one happy group and are looking forward to joining our friends in receiving our weekly wage packets! K. GOATE

FROM OLD SCHOOL TO NEW

My first impression of this school was how modern and big it was. I was very pleased to think I was going to be a pupil because my last school was prehistoric, or so we used to say. The school consisted of girls only. I was pleasantly surprised by the friendliness of the girls, when M.B. showed me round this school and joined me in a few school activities, such as the choir and the dancing class run by Mr. A. Martin. The one thing I do not like is the boys chasing the girls with frogs and other insects, apart from being terrifying, it is cruel. There are some new lessons here that I have never heard of, such as social studies, but in spite of this I think I will be very happy at this school. JACQUELINE TATE, 2B

ODE TO NATIONAL HEALTH

" My dear old boy,"	All through this
The doctor said,	The patient was quiet,
" You really must	Then in came the nurse
Be put to bed."	With his daily diet.
" You're fat as a barrel,	But as he was talking,
Your diet will help,	I'm sorry to say,
We'll start with vaccine,	The patient slowly
But try not to yelp "	Faded away.
" Your face is quite pale,	The moral to all you
Your eyes very red,	Young people I give;
Your stomach is fat	Don't be greedy
As a loaf of bread."	If you want to live.
	FRANCES ATTERBURY

14

WHERE THE MONEY GOES

Each year we carry out a survey on some aspect of pupils' lives which is not necessarily connected with school, but which they all are concerned with in some way. Previous surveys have delved into television viewing, reading habits and holidays. This year, the subject chosen is pocket money, and the results to questions asked to most forms on various aspects of this subject are given with as few comments as possible in the hope that the results in themselves will prove interesting, and possibly, surprising.

Firstly, we asked pupils to indicate the weekly amount they receive from all sources. Naturally, with ages from twelve to fifteen, these results had to be collected in years.

	Under 2/6	2/6 to 5/-	5/- to 7/6	7/6 to 10/-	Over 10/-
1st Years	73	79	24	2	1
2nd Years	28	47	32	5	6
3rd Years	11	34	23	14	24
4th Years	1	6	13	6	6

(Our Fourth Year numbers are very low this term)

Of 433 children questioned, 340 save, over half of them hoping to leave money in the bank and not draw it out for any expensive items. About one in three helps to buy clothes, and three out of four help towards holiday expenses, though in many cases, only for spending money. An interesting fact is that of the 37 children who receive over 10/- per week, only 16 of them work for it. It must be a coincidence that 35 of the 37 are in C and D forms.

Answers to the " Where do you spend most? " question

	1st Years	2nd Years	3rd Years	4th Years
Cinema and other entertainments	31	20	22	7
Tobacco	—	4	11	6
Clothes, nylons, cosmetics	—	12	18	10
Sweets, chocolates, etc.	40	38	13	3
Holidays	35	27	20	2
Hobbies and Collections	52	22	22	9
Pets	14	5	—	—

From the above details, it appears that hobbies (including record collections) take most, closely followed by sweets and chocolates, holidays and next, with still as many as 80 votes, the cinema.

The amounts in the receipts tables of course include the proceeds of part-time jobs, which 105 have. Of this group, one gives the whole of his earned money to his parents, seven give the largest half, and fifty-three give none. Many of this total of 105 receive in addition, money from parents.

Perhaps it is because this is a mixed school that only forty-six of the boys asked (over 200) have ever paid for a girl's cinema seat. No comment. IMPECUNIOUS

Overhead in a 4D English Lesson
Teacher: " Do you say adieu when you meet or leave someone? "
Pupil: (Emphatically): " I always say " ow do " when I meet a friend."

15

ROGER MARLOW, 1ST IN THE 200 YARDS SPRINT. DISTRICT SPORTS, 1959

ROGER MARLOW RECEIVES HIS PRIZE AT SCHOOL PRIZE GIVING, 1959
ROGER WOULD GO ON TO MANAGE THE HIGHLY SUCCESSFUL SUPERVISION

MR NICKERSON'S CLASS, JUNIORS, 1960

MR NIX'S CLASS, JUNIORS, CIRCA 1960

Kettering and District Schools' Athletic Association.

Certificate

Awarded to P. Green *for gaining*

FIRST

Place in Event No. 18. Throwing the Discus *for Girls under* 15

years of age, at the Annual Sports Meeting held at the Grammar School Field, Kettering.

Signed,

W. H. Witchell

Chairman.

3rd June, 1960.

PE

My favourite subject apart from English. I never got into the netball team because I was too small. I never got into the hockey team because I wasn't in the A or B class. But I was good at tennis! I remember one day the PE teacher, whose name I can't remember (I know there was a Mrs Martin who was about 4'10" and as wide) but it wasn't her, well, we were told we were to go cross-country running. We went down the playing fields and somehow got into the fields the other side the stream and were told we were to run all the way to the main road by Wicksteeds. Half way there my best friend Kathy and I decided it was too wet and cold (well we were only in blouses and navy blue knickers don't forget) so living in Cheyne Walk I knew a way over the stream further along and we decided to take a short-cut, then head back along Windmill Avenue............never pays to cheat does it - there she was on her bike, in her warm tracksuit at the top of Windmill Avenue and Pebbleford Road. Caught like moths in a car headlamp. I think we had to report to Mr Brittle about that.

The other thing in PE was THOSE BLOODY SHOWERS!!! I don't know about you boys, but we had to leave our towels at one end and walk all the way through and out the other end to collect the towels there. This wouldn't be allowed today would it? I'm sure there would be some Child Protection Regulation which would prevent this happening.

NEEDLEWORK

Can't remember the teachers name. I hated needlework and sewing and still do to this day but, of course, we had to do it. I still think that Woodwork would have been more useful to me as life went on. One lesson I remember we were making a 'Duster Coat' (all the fashion then). I was making such a mess of mine that I got up threw it across the room and said I didn't want a Duster Coat anyway. My punishment for the next two lessons...........was.............. not to have to do needlework of any type but in fact was told to go around the floor and pick up as many dropped needles and pins as I could find. Yippee!!! This was pure heaven for me. Mind you having said all that, I still have the pin cushion and Black Rag Doll I made in the first year Seniors but my Mum did all that work for me I seem to remember.

Domestic Science

Do you remember us girls having to carry those hugs, domestic science baskets around every week? They were the old orange boxes with metal handles and we went to the fruit shop to get them and took them home where we had to cover them with some sort of 'sticky backed plastic'. Then, in the dreaded needlework lesson we made a cover to put on the top. They were heavy, cumbersome and today the girls wouldn't been seen dead carrying those things along Windmill Avenue I bet. Highlight of my year was if my Mum let me have some money to go and buy a new piece of covering.....they joys of the early 60s eh!!!

COMMENTS FROM SUE LEE, HENRY GOTCH PUPIL, 1960

BARRY BASFORD'S,
HEAD BOY BADGE, 1960

MRS ROWLES CLASS, 1961

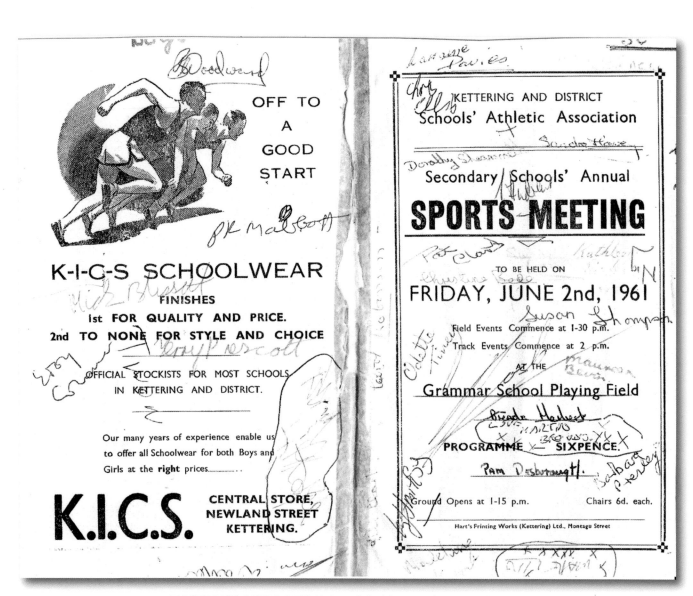

DISTRICT SCHOOL'S ATHLETICS PROGRAMME, 1961

JAVELIN, SENIOR BOYS. FINAL.

Record : J. Thorpe (Grammar) 154' 4½" (1955)

KC.	D. Leslie	GS.	R. Miller
KC.	R. Goddard	GS.	R. Tilley
		GS.	M. Staley

......2nd..................3rd.................. Distance............

JAVELIN, BOYS. FINAL.

Record : R. Crick (Rothwell) 139' 7" (1958)

SR.	K. Evans	KC.	R. Marlow
SR.	H. Arbon	RD.	C. Tomblin
HG.	R. Rivett	RD.	R. Smith
HG.	S. Dunn	GS.	R. Bruce
PC.	D. Knibbs	GS.	R. Murphy
PC.	K. Coles		

....2nd..................3rd.................. Distance.............

5. 100 YARDS, JUNIOR GIRLS. HEATS.

RD.	G. West	OL.	J. Hurry
HG.	J. Toseland	KC.	B. Murkett
HS.	L. Harvey	PC.	H. Cullum

...2nd..................3rd.................. Time............

COMPETITORS, DISTRICT SPORTS, 1961

Kettering and District Schools' Athletic Association.

Certificate

Awarded to .... P. Green .... *for gaining*

FIRST

Place in Event No 18. Throwing the Discus *for* Girls *under* 15

years of age. at the Annual Sports Meeting held at the Grammar School Field. Kettering.

Signed.

W H Witchell

Chairman.

2nd June 1961

50 YEAR JUNIOR SCHOOL REUNION, 2001
Left to Right: Back row - Yvonne Daniels, David Robinson, Richard Barratt, Brian Marshall (seated).
Front row - Lesley King, Molly Cooke (ex teacher), Sue Everitt, (inset) Kevin Ambrose (who took the photo)

SENIOR SCHOOL NETBALL TEAM, 1961

INFANT SCHOOL STAFF, CIRCA 1962

MR & MRS HART, JUNIOR SCHOOL CARETAKERS, EARLY 1960S

MRS ROWLES CLASS, JUNIORS 1962

INFANT SCHOOL PLAY, CIRCA 1962

MR NIX'S CLASS, JUNIORS 1962

THE CARETAKER'S SON, MALCOLM HART,
OUTSIDE THE CARETAKER'S HOUSE WITH PENNY THE DOG, 1962

SENIOR HOCKEY TEAM, 1962

PREFECTS, 1961-62

HENRY GOTCH SENIORS, 1962

HENRY GOTCH SENIORS, 1962

HENRY GOTCH SENIORS, 1962

HENRY GOTCH SENIORS, 1962

HENRY GOTCH INFANTS, CLASS 7, 1964

INFANT SCHOOL STAFF, SUMMER TERM, 1964

JUNIOR SCHOOL, CIRCA 1963

JUNIOR SCHOOL QUADRANGLE, 1963

MR PRIDMORE'S CLASS, CIRCA 1963

MR FRIDAY'S CLASS, CIRCA 1963

HENRY GOTCH SENIORS, 1963-64

MR HARLEY'S CLASS, 1963

MR HARLEY'S CLASS, SENIORS, 1964

1ST YEAR JUNIORS, 1964-65

MR PRIDMORE'S CLASS, SENIOR SCHOOL, 1963-64

MISS AMEY'S CLASS, CIRCA 1964

MR CORBY'S TRI-EASELS, JUNIORS 1964

28th April 1965
309 children in the
Infants. 38 children per
class.

KETTERING SCHOOL'S EASTER CONCERT

Members of Kettering Henry Gotch Junior School choir and recorder band, who gave two Easter concerts to parents and friends yesterday. The evening performance was attended by the Mayor of Kettering, Mr. L. E. Smith. The first part of the programme consisted of traditional songs from all parts of the world, and then the massed choir sang Easter hymns, while lessons were read telling the Easter story. The two events raised £10 for charity.

1965

JUNIOR SCHOOL, CIRCA 1964

SCHOOL PLAY, JUNIORS, CIRCA 1964

CLASSROOM SCENE, JUNIORS, 1965

SCHOOL PLAY, JUNIORS, CIRCA 1965

20th October 1965
Staff of all 3 schools get
together for tea and a
chat.

JUNIOR SCHOOL DINNER LADIES, CIRCA 1965

SENIOR SCHOOL PREFECTS, 1965

SENIOR SOCCER TEAM, CIRCA 1965

HENRY GOTCH JUNIORS, CIRCA 1966

SCHOOL STAFF (JUNIORS), 1966

JUNIOR SCHOOL PLAY, CIRCA 1966

2nd July 1966
Children begin swimming
in the pool for the first
time.

29th November 1966
Children take a coach to
the cinema to watch a
road safety film.

vening Telegraph, Monday, Feb. 21, 1966. 1.

J. Wykes (Henry Gotch A) wins the Kettering and District Schools Athletic Association (Under 13) cross country race at the Henry Gotch School on Saturday.

1965

JUNIOR SCHOOL PLAY, CIRCA 1966

SENIOR SCHOOL TRIP WITH MR MERCHANT, 1967

MR CORBY'S RETIREMENT, PRESENTED BY CLAUDE OGLETHORPE, CIRCA 1968

JUNIOR SCHOOL PLAY, CIRCA 1968

JUNIOR SCHOOL HALL, 1969

1939 to 1945		Miss Knight
1946 to 1950		Miss Watson
1951 to 1955 Nursery		Mrs Ullyat
		Mrs Cable
	Infants Head	Miss Molly Cooke
		Miss Cramp
		Mrs Cable
		Mrs Stimpson
		Mr Eric R Corby
	Head	Mrs Lee Evans
		Mr George Furnell "Fuzzy"
		Mrs Phyllis Hircock
		Miss Payne
		Miss Ruby Willerman
	Secondary Head	Mr Lewen
	Deputy	Miss Barr
	Music	Mr Briggs "Baldy"
		Mr Coleman
		Miss Hetherington
		Mr Johnson
		Mr Neil
		Mr Pridmore
		Mr Rosebury
		Mr Smith
		Miss Spence
1956 to 1960 As above plus: Junior		Mr Drake
		Mr Lawrence
		Miss Marlow
		Mrs Mary Rowles
		Miss Margaret Worth (Mrs Watson)

1970

13th February 1971
Decimal Day.
School dinners were 9p per meal, or 44p for a week.

21st October 1971
The Netball team beat Milbrook Junior for the first time.

2nd February 1972
All year 2 go to Milbrook for several weeks during the coal strike as the school has no coal for heat.

HENRY GOTCH INFANT STAFF, MAY 1973

26ᵗʰ June 1974
A black and white t.v. is
installed in school.

HENRY GOTCH INFANT STAFF, JUNE 1974

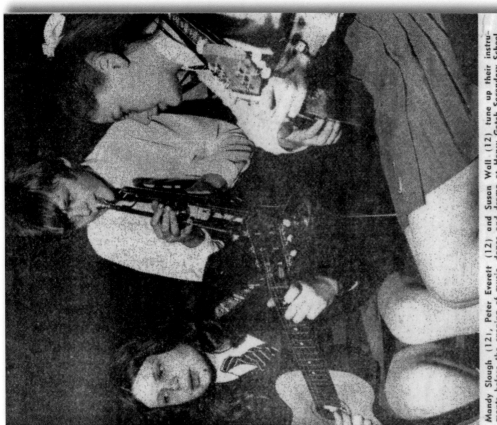

Schoolchildren entertain parents

Mandy Slough (12), Peter Everett (12) and Susan Wall (12) tune up their instruments before the evening of music, dance and drama at Henry Gotch Secondary School, Kettering, last night.

PUPILS of Henry Gotch Secondary School, Kettering, gave over 200 parents an evening of music, dance and drama last night and will repeat the show tonight.

About 130 pupils took part in the varied programme, and all the preparation for the evening had been made in their own time.

For the first 20 minutes,

the choir and instrumentalists entertained with guitars, violins, piano and brass.

Then the drama club took over and presented a short play entitled "The Mystery Parcel."

The dance club gave a performance of two national dances

1973

INFANTS, CIRCA 1975

HENRY GOTCH INFANT STAFF, 1976

HENRY GOTCH SENIOR FOOTBALL TEAM, 1976

SECRET OF THE STABLE

YOUNGSTERS from Kettering's Henry Gotch Junior School are reliving the very first Christmas with their story of the Nativity.

The play will be performed tonight at a carol concert for parents and friends of the school.

About 100 children are taking part — including the school choir, recorder players, and one of the fourth year classes which is performing the Nativity.

The rest of the school, and some of the parents, have already seen the production at a rehearsal earlier this week.

About 150 tickets have been sold for tonight's performance. "If it goes as well as the dress rehearsal I know everyone will enjoy it," said the headmaster Mr John Wholley.

● Nativity cast (from left) Lee Able, Lindsay Thurston, Paul Foster, Darren Price, Christine Hamilton, Joanne Castle, Marcus Hatton, Andrew Towell, Jane Horbatowski.

CIRCA 1977

INFANTS SPORTS DAY, CIRCA 1978

MRS BITHRAY'S CLASS, INFANTS, 1978

Left to Right: Back row - Mrs Bithray, Joane Catchpole, Faye Sherratt, Keith Mathews, Peter Elmore, Heidi, Darren Price, Marcus Hatton, Julie Robertson, Cheryl Thurston, Lee, Britt Wells, Alison Jones, Mrs Peasley (Headmistress).
Middle row - Barbara Chapman, Melanie, Ashley Scott, Sally Meagan, Manjeet, Theresa Hartnett, Robert Pizamenti, Lisa.
Front row - Emma Benton, James Craxford, Debbie Liggins, Karl Forster, Jamie Smallman, Sharon Politis, Roseanna Mills.

1st May 1978
The school shuts for the
first ever May bank
holiday.

FIRE DISPLAY, CIRCA LATE 70S

CLASS OF '78 REUNION, NOVEMBER 2010, THE BEESWING

PUPILS BLOWN OFF COURSE

IT WAS a race against the wind at the annual sports day at Henry Gotch Infants' School, Kettering.

Blustery weather meant that in the egg and spoon race some of the eggs were blown from their spoons. Our picture (right) shows some of the competitors.

About 250 parents and friends turned out to watch the sports. They went back in the afternoon for the annual family picnic in the school grounds.

Headmistress Mrs Joyce Peasley said: "It was all very enjoyable despite the weather."

She thanked everyone who supported the events, included parents and staff who made the picnic food.

INFANT SCHOOL SPORTS, CIRCA 1979

MRS CURTIS INFANTS CLASS, CIRCA 1979
Mrs Peasley (Head) on front left

INFANT SCHOOL STAFF, 1979

4th September 1979
Mr Drew starts teaching
at Henry Gotch.

6th November 1979
The school nurse inspects
the children's hair.

SCHOOL CHOIR AND ORCHESTRA, CIRCA 1979

SCHOOLS TAKE TO THE TRACK

● Skipping to first place in the third year race is nine-year-old Kirsty Hamilton.

Running into rain

YOUNGSTERS at a Kettering school had their sports day between bouts of rain.

Headmaster of Henry Gotch Junior School Mr John Wholley said: "We had to start a bit later than planned but we managed to finish before the rain started again."

to 11-year-olds took part in the 53 events which included obstacle, sack and relay races, and a tug-of-war.

About 200 parents turned out to watch the afternoon's activities at the school's playing field on Thursday.

The winning team, Ise House, was presented with

the House Cup by the chairman of the school managers, Mr E A Crayford.

The results were Ise first with 146 points, Welland second with 140, Slade third with 132 and Nene fourth with 114.

Mr Wholley said: "Ise haven't won for about four years so the children were very pleased."

1979

SENIOR FOOTBALL TEAM, 1979

2nd April 1980
The school canteen closes and dinners are delivered from Henry Gotch school (now Ise).

EVENING TELEGRAPH, Friday, June 20, 1980

Girls pull their weight in sports

A MIXED tug-o-war team was one of the highlights at the Henry Gotch Junior School annual sports day in Kettering.

Headmaster Mr John Wholley said; "They have to have an equal number in each team, there is no sex bias in this sport.

"Everything went very smoothly, the way it is supposed to go. The sun came out at lunchtime and about 200 parents and friends of the school came along to watch."

All 285 pupils at the school took part in the sports for the four different houses — Nene, Welland, Ise and Slade.

At the end of the afternoon, Nene House came out on top with 151 points and were presented with the E A Timson Cup by Mrs Lorraine Foster, a parent governor at the school.

Races for the pupils included egg and spoon, obstacle, sack, skipping and relay.

Mr Wholley said: "The track was marked out in the morning by county ground staff and four parents acted as judges."

● Pupils take the strain.

JUNIOR SCHOOL

INFANT NATIVITY PLAY, CIRCA 1980

HENRY GOTCH INFANT SCHOOL STAFF, 1980

HENRY GOTCH INFANT SCHOOL STAFF, 1981

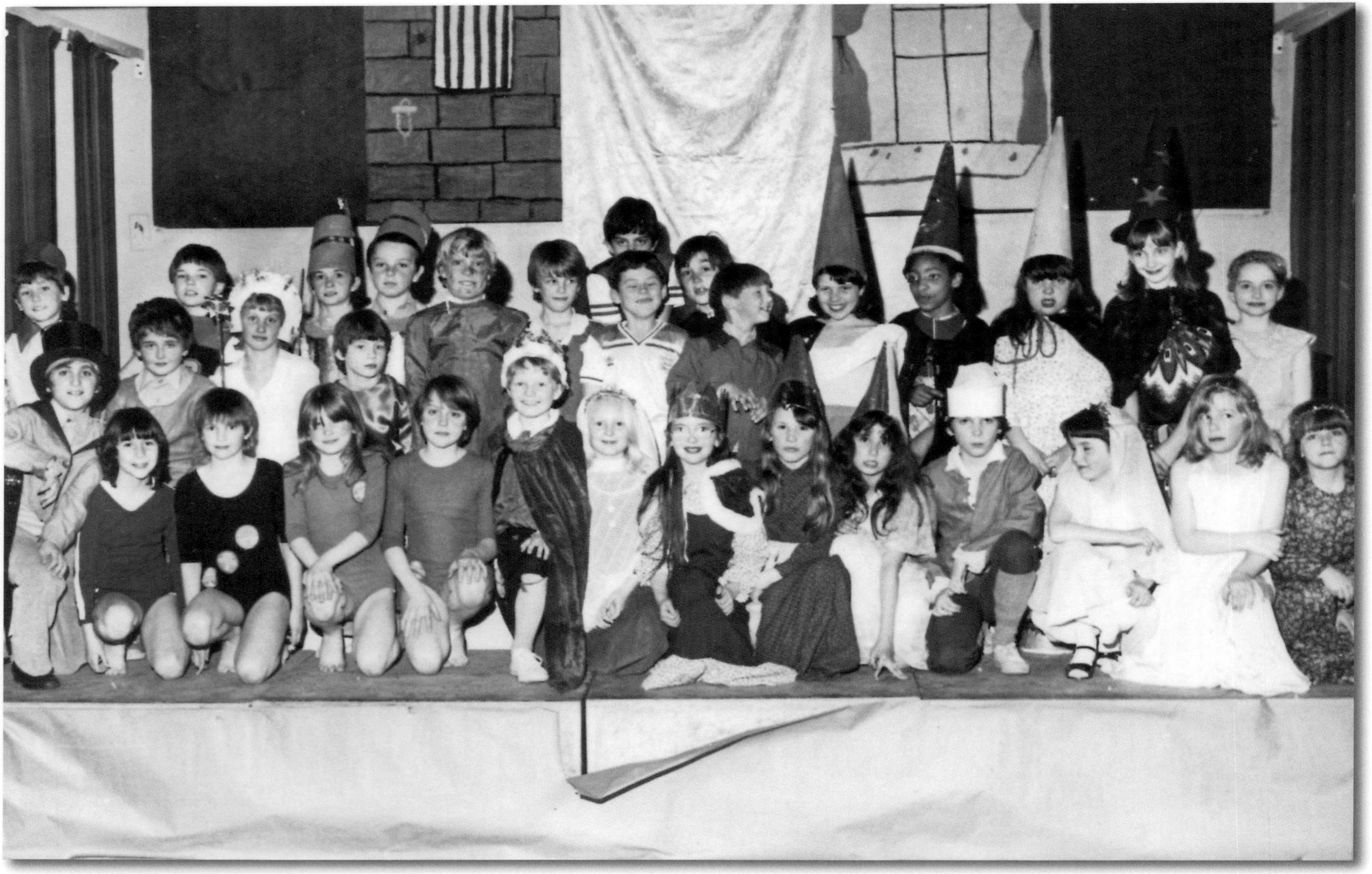

JUNIOR SCHOOL NATIVITY PLAY, 1981

CELEBRATING PRINCE CHARLES & DIANA'S WEDDING,
JUNIOR SCHOOL PLAY, 1981

HENRY GOTCH SENIORS NETBALL TEAM, CIRCA 1981

INFANTS, 1982

HENRY GOTCH INFANTS, CLASS 3, 2-7-1982

INFANT NATIVITY PLAY, 1982

INFANTS & JUNIOR SCHOOL CANTEEN DEMOLISHED, CIRCA 1982/3

THE OLD UNIFORM AND SCHOOL CANTEEN

1st January 1982
Mr Toon begins teaching at Henry Gotch.

1st September 1982
All children aged 4 and above start Nursery in September from now on. Before that they started the term after their birthday.

22nd October 1982
Mr Drew and Mr Toon take their classes into town to use computer.

BREAKING UP FOR SUMMER HOLIDAYS, JUNIORS 1982

HENRY GOTCH JUNIORS RUNNERS UP,
PRIMARY SCHOOL SOCCER LEAGUE, 1982-3

HENRY GOTCH SENIOR STAFF FOOTBALL TEAM, 1982

HALF A SIXPENCE CAST, 1982

MRS BITHRAY'S CLASS 3, JUNE 1983
Mrs Peasley (Head) on front left

INFANTS NATIVITY PLAY, 1983

23rd September 1983
The first computer
arrives in school for use
by pupils.

INFANT SCHOOL SPORTS DAY, 1983

HENRY GOTCH INFANT SCHOOL STAFF, APRIL 1983

SENIOR SCHOOL PRODUCTION, HALF A SIXPENCE, 1983

4th September 1984
Mrs Stokes begins work
in the office.

HENRY GOTCH JUNIORS NETBALL TEAM,
25-3-1983
Left to Right: Back row - Faye Sherrat, Britt Wells,
Mrs Loveridge (Teacher), Sadie Bagsy, Jane Horbatowski
Front row - Debbie Burton, Katie Marlow, Christine Hamilton

HENRY GOTCH INFANTS STAFF, 31-3-1983

RIDING TALL

Jane calls the shots!

THE colourful character of Calamity Jane was brought to life this week by Kettering pupil Patricia O'Donnell when she took the lead role in her school's latest production.

Patricia, a sixth-former at Henry Gotch School, is no newcomer to acting, having played Dorothy when her school staged The Wizard of Oz and Eliza Doolittle in My Fair Lady.

She and the rest of the cast had been rehearsing since September for the musical, which opened on Wednesday and ends its run tonight.

Calamity is pictured here with Wild Bill Hickok, played by Trevor Phillips.

SENIOR SCHOOL PRODUCTION, CALAMITY JANE, 1984

HENRY GOTCH SCHOOL

PRESENTS

CALAMITY JANE

WED THURS FRI
18th 19th 20th
JANUARY '84.
7.00 PM

ENTRY BY PROGRAMME.
PRICE £1.00.

AVAILABLE AT SCHOOL OFFICE
OR ON THE DOOR.

SPECIAL RATES AVAILABLE FOR
GROUPS. SENIOR CITIZENS. CHILDRE

CAST

Calamity Jane	Patricia O'Donnell
Wild Bill Hickock	Trevor Phillips
Danny Gilmartin	Lee Orbell
Katie Brown	Sonya Payne
Henry Miller	Carlo Fiorentino
Susan	Maria Sykes
Francis Fryer	Jonathan Shipton
Adelaide Adams	Lesley Arbon
Doc Pierce	Darren Turner
Joe	Graham Kinchin
Charlie	David Hopkins
Hank	Spencer Gilbert
Pete	James Aston
Colonel	Mark Fountain
Stagecoach Passengers	Della Hill, Rachel Emery
Cowboys	Gordon Brigstock
	Darren Arbon
	Martyn Lund
	Andrew Clarke
	Andrew Cosford
Townswomen	Dawn Cooper
	Darlene Hill
	Sallyann Johnson
	Sarah Robinson
	Denise Sinclair
	Kerry Moore
	Sharon Bedford

Saloon Girls	Jane Miller
	Clare Miller
	Emma Smith
	Claire Tilley
	Vicky Tingle
	Heidi Montgomery
Adelaide's Admirers	Helen Sykes
	Shella Mullen
	Kim Harrison
	Shelley Turner
	Beverley Chapman
	Jackie Scarfe
	Denise Williamson
	Barbara Chamberlain
Soldiers	Alison Coldicott
	Lisa O'Dell
	Ann Scott
	Dawn Shatford
	Cheryl Szoltysek
Wives	Kerry Bates
	Karen O'Dell
	Angela Jenkins
	Michelle Atkinson
	Paula Chamberlain
Bridesmaids	Cara Hill
	Andrea Bevin
	Lisa Barker
	Kim McAlwane
	Sam Taylor
	Ann Radford

Musicians	Flutes	Helen Williamson
		Deborah Stone
	Violin	Vicky Mogridge
	Cello	Karen Underwood
	Trumpet	John Dunk
	Horn	Belinda Coltman
	Clarinet	Susan Tingle

VIOLA LORNA FISKE. BASS ROBERT KEARLEY. TROMBONE DAVID GIBBS

Six of the best

YOUNGSTERS from a Kettering school have won the chance to represent the district in a county football championship.

For the first time a team from Henry Gotch Junior School has won a six-a-side tournament and taken the Ken Burton Shield.

The winners are pictured (from left) Marc Andrews, Ashley Scott, Christopher Munns, Mark Storey, Keith Massie and Mark Grove (reserve). Goalkeeper Adam Shaw is missing.

Three other schools took part in the finals of the

Kettering and Corby junior schools' tournament. They were St Brendan's and Danesholme, Corby, and Barton Seagrave.

All the teams played each other at Barton Seagrave, with two points for a win and one for a draw.

The shield was presented by Mr Brian Pack, chairman of the Kettering and Corby Junior Schools Football Association.

The youngsters from Henry Gotch will represent the district in the county competition, which will be played early next year.

HENRY GOTCH JUNIOR SCHOOL,
6-A-SIDE CHAMPIONS, 1985

15th April 1985
Mrs Cuthbert starts.

HENRY GOTCH JUNIOR SCHOOL,
6-A-SIDE CHAMPIONS, 1985

Team is top of league — at last!

• The Junior Football League top team — (front) Nathan Eady, Mark Grove, Mark Storey, John Stewart, Chris Muns; (rear) Marc Andrews, Stuart Peasnall, Keith Massie, Martin Rivett, Ashley Scott, Adam Shaw, Terry West.

YOUNGSTERS from a Kettering school have finally won a football trophy that has eluded them for 36 years.

The Kettering and District Junior Football League started in 1948 and Henry Gotch Junior School has just won division one.

Headmaster Mr John Wholley said: "The pupils are coached by David Drew and he has done a jolly good job.

"I am hoping we shall see the school's name on the trophy a bit more often now."

The school has also won a six-a-side tournament at Millbrook School, Kettering, in competition with 13 other teams from the area and at the end of last year won the Kettering and Corby district six-a-side contest.

All the pupils from Henry Gotch who took part in the competitions have received an inscribed medal.

EVENING TELEGRAPH ARTICLE
HENRY GOTCH JUNIORS,
CHAMPIONS, 1985

10th July 1985
School bookshop started.

THE GIRLS, SUMMER 1985

HENRY GOTCH JUNIORS, LEAGUE WINNERS, 1985

Couple's farewell

HEADMASTER John Wholley and his wife Kathleen have packed away their school books for the last time after 14 years together at the helm of Henry Gotch Juniors, Kettering.

Mr Wholley, 60, has been head since 1971 and Mrs Wholley, 60, began running the school office a year later. They were showered with retirement gifts, including two suitcases from the children.

Now the couple, of Kipling Road, are looking forward to developing their other interests. He plans to master chess and learn to cook and she will increase her voluntary work and enjoy WI and Kettering Flower Arrangement Club meetings.

They are pictured with their gifts, surrounded by pupils.

The couple married 35 years ago when Mr Wholley left the RAF, having served abroad,

including Singapore and India, during World War Two. They have two sons, teacher Peter and solicitor Richard, and two grandchildren with two more due this summer.

Mr Wholley said: "There have been two major changes since I joined Henry Gotch — the number of pupils has dropped from 340 to 250 and far fewer go home for lunch."

Other heads in the area gave the couple a set of electronic scales and past and present staff and governors presented a table, saucepans and bouquet at a farewell party. Children and staff at Henry Gotch Infants School handed over a pen.

And, in return, Mr Wholley bought his pupils a book about birds and re-stocked the fish pond which had been badly hit by the cold winter.

He is to be succeeded by Mr Ian Nelson, who is moving from Overstone Primary School.

7th April 1986

1986

SENIOR BASKETBALL TEAM, 1985

SENIOR FOOTBALL TEAM, 1985

SENIOR BASKETBALL TEAM, 1985

FAME IS ON THE CARDS . . .

YOUNG Christmas card designers at Kettering's Henry Gotch School have surprised management at a local firm with their expertise.

As part of Industry Year the school linked up with Haverhill Generators, of Telford Way, Kettering, and as Christmas approached the firm challenged young artists to design a Christmas card.

The pupils were told to use the firm's product linked with the seasonal theme, with the winner being used by Haverhill as its company card to send to its contacts.

Marcus Bird, 15, won the competition with his design, with Gordon Brigstock, 16, Dale Bates, 14, and Ashley Scott, 14 as runners-up.

Haverhill director Philip Wayman, visited the school to hand out the prizes, £10 to the winners and £5 to the runners-up.

He said: "The standard was brilliant, the winner's card has been printed 5,000 times and will now be used as the company's card."

Headmaster John Howard said: "It's been a very useful link with the firm, culminating in the competition. Marcus's card was superb. We were very proud of his entry."

● Marcus receives his prize from Mr Wayman watched by Mr Howard and (from left) Gordon, Ashley and Dale.

1986

NETBALL TRAINING SESSION, 1985/86
Centre Back: Paula Conde who played for England Schools

HENRY GOTCH SCHOOL
Deeble Road
KETTERING
Northants
NN15 7AA

Tel. No.
Kett. 513770

Headteacher: J. C. HOWARD   B.D.

Deputy Head: L. R. CRABB   B.Sc.,

Deputy Head: J. S. BLESSETT   LL.B.,A.I.L.,

Deputy Head: B. H. ABLETT   Cert. Ed.

SENIOR SCHOOL STAFF, 1986

Henry Gotch School

I always thought of science as dissecting frogs on the first lesson, so I was quite worried. But I think science is my best subject now.

I feel at home here now because I know lots more people than when I started here. The teachers know me and are much kinder.

Henry Gotch is a lot different from a junior school. At a senior school you go from class to class for different subjects.

It takes you only 2 or 3 weeks to learn the school time table.

I think... I knew... first thing...

I thought it would be like Grange Hill but it is not.

I feel as though I am at home at school because some teachers are proud and they are ready to help you. You have different teaching for different subjects.

My advice for a new pupil is this: they should not worry. I was worried someone would hit me or someone older. My head saw me at the end & I told them I had. That at the end of... "It's not so bad."

I was really shy and nervous and when I'd come here and because I hadn't gone to school in Kettering I didn't know many. But I made friends easily and I'm sure you will if you are starting too knowing anyone.

... looking forward to coming to Kut day I was shy but I am in the class, I can make friends before I did in my...

I do feel at home here now because you first get to know everybody in the year. And somewhere in the second year. And I know all the homes and classrooms and I know where all they are.

Henry Gotch seemed bigger than my junior school but after a while it seemed much small.

When I first arrived I thought it was really difficult but now they seem easier than...

When you come into the school you'll think 'Oh will I find your way around all the classrooms and how...' a week you get used to it and...

I think I've had a good year. The first day I was really scared. But as the weeks went on I didn't feel so scared.

PUPIL'S INFORMATION BOOKS, 1986

1986

PROSPECTUS 1986/87

Henry Gotch School

Careers Guidance

The programme of careers guidance begins in the Third Year and continues until pupils leave school, whether at 16, 17 or 18. In addition to the careers teacher, the Pastoral staff are also involved with the County Youth Employment Service and Careers Officers regularly visit the school to talk to pupils. The Careers Suite is well equipped and contains a vast quantity of literature. It is staffed during lunch periods, and is available to all pupils seeking advice and information.

Lifeskills

During their five years all pupils follow a course in lifeskills. This will help them to acquire skills necessary for the transfer from school to work and adulthood. Underpinning a great deal of this work is the cultivation of an aware, sensitive stance to life in the twentieth century and the gaining of moral sensibilities. Groups will be small (about 15 pupils) to enable discussion and visits. During their programme, in which both Form Tutors and specialist staff will be involved, tutors and students will work together to develop a profile of the pupils contribution to, and progress in, school.

The Curriculum

The school aims to provide all children with a curriculum of balance, depth and breadth. To this end all pupils engage in a common core curriculum for five years.

All pupils follow courses in English, Languages, Maths, Humanities, Science, Design and Recreational and Performing Arts (R.P.A.).

ENGLISH	–	English – literature and language
MATHS	–	Mathematics – skills, concepts and language
HUMANITIES	–	A synoptic study of man and his environment using the disciplines of history, geography, religion and moral education (Humanities)
DESIGN	–	The designing, making and producing of artefacts and ideas using arts, crafts and technology (Design)
SCIENCE	–	A balanced approach encompassing the disciplines of physics, chemistry and biology
R.P.A.	–	Recreational and Performing Arts skills using music, drama, dance and physical education
LANGUAGE	–	The skills of oral and written work in German and French
EXTENSION STUDIES	–	All pupils have the opportunity in each subject area of extending their studies. This, while allowing a degree of specialisation, enables students to tailor their overall curriculum to their own needs by introducing considerable elements of choice.

8

9

SOME OF THE SENIOR SCHOOL RULES, 1986

CLASS PHOTO, CIRCA 1986

SCHOOL EVENTS

8th November to 15th November 1986 - Longtown trip for 4th & 5th yrs.
10th December - Dance Evening 5th yr. 7.00 p.m.
11th to 12th December 1986 - Kidnapped at Xmas - School Production
13th December - RPA Music Evening 7.00 p.m.
17th December to 24th December 1986 - Skiing Trip

EXAMINATION, PARENTS EVENINGS AND REPORTS

21st October 1986 - Interim Parents Evening for Year 1
4th November 1986 - Interim Parents Evening for Year 2
13th November 1986 - Interim Parents Evening for Years 3 & 6
1st December 1986 - Interim Parents Evening for Year 4
1st - 5th December 1986 - Year 5 Practice Exams

CONSULTATIVE MEETINGS

School Committee Meetings :
9th October   12.30 p.m.
20th November 12.30 p.m.
12th December 12.30 p.m.

PARENTS AND FRIENDS OF HENRY GOTCH

6th October 1986 - AGM 7.30 p.m.
13th October 1986 - PSA Committee Meeting 7.30 p.m.
18th October 1986 - Jumble Sale 2.00 p.m.
3rd November 1986 - PSA Committee Meeting 7.30 p.m.
22nd November 1986 - Barn Dance
1st December 1986 - PSA Committee Meeting 7.30 p.m.
6th December 1986 - PSA Christmas Fair

TERM DATES 1986

GCSE Training Day - Thursday 23rd October 1986
School Closed
Autumn Half Term - Close Friday 24th October
Re-open Monday 3rd November
Christmas - Close Friday 19th December 1986
Spring Term - Re-open Wednesday 7th January 1987

HENRY GOTCH SCHOOL KETTERING

AUTUMN TERM 1986

SPORTS FIXTURES	SOCCER		
8th September 1986	Under 16	Beanfield	HG
11th September 1986	Under 15	Beanfield	HG
15th September 1986	Under 13	Kingswood	A
15th September 1986	Under 15 (Cup)	Kingswood	HG
17th September 1986	Under 16	Queen Elizabeth	A
18th September 1986	Under 14	Kingswood	A
22nd September 1986	Under 16	Montsaye	A
25th September 1986	Under 13	Beanfield	A
29th September 1986	Under 13	Montsaye	A
2nd October 1986	Under 15	Kingswood	A
9th October 1986	Under 15	Montsaye	A
13th October 1986	Under 15	Queen Elizabeth	HG
14th October 1986	Under 14	Beanfield	HG
16th October 1986	Under 15	Lodge Park	HG
20th October 1986	Under 13	Lodge Park	A
21st October 1986	Under 14	Montsaye	A
22nd October 1986	Under 16	Lodge Park	HG
4th March 1987	Under 13	Queen Elizabeth	A
5th March 1987	Under 15	Bishop Stopford	A
9th March 1987	Under 12	Kettering Boys	HG
9th March 1987	Under 14	Kettering Boys	HG
11th March 1987	Under 13	Kettering Boys	HG
11th March 1987	Under 15	Kettering Boys	HG
17th March 1987	Under 13	Montagu	HG
17th March 1987	Under 15	Montagu	HG
19th March 1987	Under 14	Montagu	HG
26th March 1987	Under 14	Bishop Stopford	A
30th March 1987	Under 14	Queen Elizabeth	HG

SPORTS FIXTURES	NETBALL & HOCKEY	
20th September 1986	U16 County Hockey Trials	
22nd September 1986	2/Sen. Netball	Bishop St. H
24th September 1986	Lower School Hockey	Bishop St. A
27th September 1986	U18 County Hockey Trials	
29th September 1986	Netball	Southfield
1st October 1986	Hockey 2/3	Southfield
6th October 1986	Netball Our Lady + Pope John	
7th October 1986	2nd Year/Sen. Netball District Tournament at Montsaye	
8th October 1986	Hockey 2/3 Our Lady + Pope John	
13th October 1986	Netball	Latimer
14th October 1986	3rd Year/Sen. Netball District Tournament at Southfield	
16th October 1986	Hockey 2/3	Latimer
20th October 1986	Netball	Montagu
22nd October 1986	Hockey 2/3	Montagu
8th November 1986	U14, U16, U18 County Netball Trials	
17th November 1986	1st Year Netball	Bishop St.
17th November 1986	1st Year Hockey	Bishop St.
24th November 1986	1st Year Netball	Our Lady
24th November 1986	1st Year Hockey	Our Lady
1st December 1986	1st Year Netball	Southfield
1st December 1986	1st Year Hockey	Southfield
6th December 1986	U15/1st XI County Hockey Tournaments	
8th December 1986	1st Year Netball	Montsaye
8th December 1986	1st Year Hockey	Montsaye

SPORTS FIXTURES	CROSS-COUNTRY/ATHLETICS	
2nd October 1986	Cross Country	Latimer
15th October 1986	Cross Country	Montagu
13th December 1986	District Cross Country	Henry Gotch
31st January 1987	County Cross Country	Spomne
12th May 1987	Athletics Trials	Kettering Boys
2nd June 1987	Yr. 2 Athletic Champ.	Kettering Boys
9th June 1987	Yr. 1 Athletic Champ.	Montsaye
16th June 1987	Yr. 3 Athletic Champ.	Bishop Stopford

SENIOR SCHOOL PROGRAMME, 1986

The Headmaster. Mr Howard.

Mr Howard's office is next to the school office on the first floor. You are most likely to meet him in assembly or in the canteen at lunch.

Deputy Head Mr Crabb

Mr Crabb teaches Maths

Deputy Head Mr Blessit

Mr Blessit teaches Modern Languages.

Deputy Head Mr Ablett

Mr Ablett teaches Maths.

Senior Year Tutor Mr Railton.

Mr Railton is in charge of the well-being of all those in the lower school.
He can be found in the Lower School office.
He teaches Science.

Year Tutor Mrs Tunnicliff.

Mrs Tunnicliff works with Mr Railton looking after lower school pupils. She teaches PE.

School Bursar Mrs Conway.

Mrs Conway looks after the school office. You must report to this office if you arrive late or have to sign out for a medical appointment.

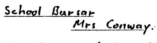

Stop Press
Mr Ludbrook also helps to look after lower school pupils.

SENIOR TEACHERS, 1986
MRS CONWAY DEFACED BY ROBIN SELLERS

CLASS 3, 1987/88

SUPERSCHOOLS SUPERSTARS, MR HOWARD & BRIAN HOOPER, 1987

CHRISTMAS, 1988

CLASS 3, 1988/89

5th September 1988
School closed to pupils
for first ever teacher
training day (Baker day).

The golden years at Henry Gotch

Do you recognise anyone on this school photo?

Head teachers of the Henry Gotch Infant and Junior schools discuss the history of the schools

The Henry Gotch school sign will stir up many happy memories for former and present day pupils

EVENING TELEGRAPH ARTICLE, CIRCA 1988

T'S YOUR SCHOOL

HEAD WORK... Deirde Sneath helps nie Pike, 6, and Andrew Goode, 7, with ir technical kit

■ PUPIL POWER... There's plenty to smile about at Henry Gotch Infants

Hooray Henry Gotch

Story by Deborah Henderson
Pictures by Alison Bagley

ACT FILE

AME OF SCHOOL: Henry otch Infant School.

DDRESS: Windmill Avenue, ettering.

EAD TEACHER: Deidre neath.

UMBER OF TEACHERS: Six ant School teachers and one rsery School teacher.

UMBER OF PUPILS: 165 ints and 152 nursery school-ildren.

GE RANGE: Three to seven ar-olds.

CHOOL COLOURS: Maroon d grey.

I NEVER believed the saying that schooldays where the happiest days of your life until I met head teacher Deidre Sneath.

Deidre took over the running of Henry Gotch Infant School in Kettering in January 1985.

"I had a phone call from a lady in Corby who told me her relative in Australia wanted to know when the school was holding its 50th anniversary celebrations," she said.

"Apparently the Australian lady used to go to the Infant School and she intends to travel all the way from Australia to be here for our celebrations.

"I think that is marvellous. This good lady said she wouldn't miss our celebrations for anything."

There is a definite air of excitement already at the school as plans are being made to throw a special bash to mark 50 years next summer.

Deidre, 52, added: "It's a joint celebration with the Junior School. We're hoping to get a Royal princess or the Duchess of York to plant a tree or something.

"We'll be holding an exhibition and we are arranging for former pupils to bring in their old photographs of the school.

"We had many war-time evacuees at the school and we are hoping that they will be able to come along to help us celebrate."

Deidre, who has been in the teaching profession since 1956, seems to have a boundless energy which is not only geared to special events but also to the day-to-day running of the school.

She said: "We aim to provide a happy caring environment for the children. What's special about this school is that you see them growing up. From the nursery they join the Infants and then go on to the Junior school and then to the secondary. After all that many of them come back as adults to take up evening classes."

Deidre said they had few rules but admitted one rule was quite unusual. The children are not allowed to eat sweets during playtime. They are encouraged to bring in a piece of fruit.

"The junk food ban was my predecessor's idea and when I joined the school I noticed the staff and parents were proud of their good record.

"The rule was so well established that I decided to maintain it. I suppose you could call us fruit and nut case."

The school consists of 165 infants and 152 part-time nursery children. Deidre says she tries to encourage

participation in the Technical Toy area which helps the children develop design skills.

She said: "I believe this to be an important part of their education. I encourage the girls just as much as the boys to try and build something here.

"When these children leave school they will be surrounded with technology everywhere they go so it's best to get them started at an early age."

And Deidre's attempts certainly seem to have paid off because most of the children I spoke to said they wanted to become engineers after leaving school.

Young Andrew Goode and Jamie Pyke had a very clear sighted view of how they would spend the rest of their lives.

Six-year-old Jamie, who was helping Andrew, seven, build a robot said: "When I grow up I shall become a builder but in my spare time I will design a racing car and then I will become a full-time racing driver."

And Andrew said: "I will become a full-time footballer and a part-time engineer. I like maths and I want to be able to make more robots."

Deidre pointed out a tiny 10ft by 8ft kitchen where she said 200 dinners were made daily during the war when the school was flooded with evacuees. Nowadays the children use the dining facilities at the junior school.

And teacher Irene Bithray remembered the time several years ago when the children had to take their lessons at Millbrook School when it became impossible to heat Henry Gotch during the coal strike.

Deidre said: "I think all the teachers enjoy Christmas when the children from the senior school perform their Christmas concert. The little ones also take part and everyone dresses up.

"The children in need group gave us a marvellous garden bench, a bird bath and sun dial for our garden. If I had my life over again and could chose a school to go to I would have to chose this one."

Jean.

In House Magazine

Henry Gotch Staff

October 1988

Issue 1. Volume 1.

SECOND YEAR VISIT TO GRANDCAMP.NORMANDY.4th.to 8th.JULY 19 School visits are a feature of school life almost impossible to escape,but viewed either with enthusiasm or dread ! Brian's account reveals that he trod a middle road, with sense of humour intact!

The Gotch party boarded the bus during the early hours of Monday 4th. July. Alf, our driver from sunny Scunny, took us to Brackley for the remaining pupils and staff, a motor-way cafe and on to Portsmouth, for the crossing on the Brittany ferry, the Gotland. Many queasy hours later, after a very rough crossing, we docked at Oustreham, arriving at Grandcamp and our hotel, some two hours later.

On Tuesday the group visited a French market, Arromanche, to see the concrete pontoons from D-day and the Pointe du Hoc (The Longest Day).Here Anthony Tibbets, defending the cliffs from the attacking American Rangers, sustained a fractured arm, while leaping around the sheltered gun emplacements.The afternoon visit to the Battle of Normandy museum was also educational as the Gotch pupils attempted to succeed where the Germans failed by dismembering an American Sherman tank!

That evening, around midnight, the local siren aroused the already wide-awake hotel. Without exception, everyone left their rooms and paraded up and down the corridor in a state of high excitement.Some two hours later all had settled down and the party leader was able to return to his bed.(Some pupils actually complained about having to stand bare foot on a stone tiled floor at one o'clock in the morning!)

The next morning the sun shone, the wind howled, the sea-weed smelled and everyone,vigourously encouraged, went to take part in a jolly game on the beach; the high spot being the rounder's match between a team of male staff and girls against numerically superior boys.After liberal interpretation of the rules, the staff and girls scored five and a half rounders. The game was then suspended, the boys were promised their innings later.

After a lunch of les petits crabs, we left for Mont St.Michael, where we managed, for a little while, to elude our charges and see the crowded streets and jumbled buildings as ordinary tourists.Our packed evening meal followed at the side of the main road on two small picnic tables, where we all enjoyed our foot long sandwiches, bottled water-without cups-and Golden Delicious apples. The journey home was uneventful apart from a slight delay of twenty minutes, whilst a few thousand sheep crossed the road in front of us.

During the late evening, Neil Overson, whilst attempting to open a small bottle, managed to cut the base of his thumb and spread blood over his bedroom.After a lengthy debate, it was decided to dress the wound with antiseptic cream, butterfly stitches and bandage.The next morning the doctor prescribed four necessary medications and a tetanus injection to be given by a visiting nurse. He reluctantly agreed that the first aid alone would do!

A further evening vigil ended for the staff at 12¦45 a.m.-only six pupils having bared their feet on the corridor floor!

6.

MRS BITHRAY'S INFANTS CLASS, CIRCA 1989

STAFF, 1989

JULY 1989

Left to Right: Hayley McCarthy, Kimberley Foster, Rachel Swan, Marie Blades, Richard Gilbert, Andrew Towning

Teacher: Mrs Bithray

HENRY GOTCH SCHOOL IS 50 TODAY!

Our school is 50 today
Our school is happy this way
People come and people go
It just seems like a day ago
Small and afraid I came to this school.

It's five to nine in the morning
The bell rings, the register's called
Later we line up and quiet
For when we enter the hall

Our school is 50 today ....

Sometimes the work is easy
Other times it is hard
Sometimes the time passes quickly
Other times it seems to drag on and on, on and on

Our school is 50 today ....

Now and again we are angels
Helping each other all day
Next we behave like devils
Pushing and fighting and generally making a noise.

Our school is 50 today ....

You hear a big cheer when the bell goes
Grabbing our coats and our bags
We all run out to the playground
To meet our mums and our dads

Our school is 50 today
Our school is happy this way
People come and people go
It just seems like a day ago
Small and afraid I came to this school.

Written by the children assisted by Mr J. Miller

1989

COLLAGE OF SCHOOL BY MRS LOVERIDGE, 1989

School Organisation

School times are —   8.55 a.m. to 11.55 a.m.   1.10 p.m. to 3.40 p.m.

We expect children to be neatly dressed and there is school uniform comprising grey skirt/pinafore dress or trousers/shorts with white blouse or grey shirt and grey cardigan/pullover. School ties can be obtained from Chalkleys Ltd. in Silver Street.

For P.E. we prefer each child to have a leotard/shorts/tee shirt and plimsolls and for Games shorts/tee shirt and plimsolls/trainers. A tracksuit or jumper is advisable for the colder weather.

An old shirt or apron is needed for painting and craft lessons.

In order to avoid an accumulation of lost property all clothing should be named. Name tags can be ordered through school; see the secretary for details.

School meals are available at the current rate payable on the first day of the week. Children are able to bring packed lunches but glass containers and canned drinks are not allowed. Children are not allowed to eat at break times or in the main school building.

Discipline and good behaviour is expected of all children and serious lapses will be notified to the parents as they occur. Corporal punishment is not used in the school in accordance with a policy introduced by the Education Committee and as now required by the Education (No. 2) Act 1986.

Children's pastoral and medical welfare is a matter for individual attention. If a child becomes unwell in school parents are notified in order that they may collect their child. For this reason we need to be able to contact parents during the school day and appreciate a telephone number to allow us to do so. If a child requires medication parents are able to use the office to administer it.

All absences should be notified by either telephone or letter.

Homework is not generally set but children are asked to learn spellings/tables at home. Parents are encouraged to hear their children read and to read to them. It is not the policy to set homework for children absent from school through illness or a family holiday.

At the moment all our classes are mixed ability and some have children from two age ranges.

1989

MRS MOSSOP, MRS SNEATH (HEAD), MRS DREDGE, CIRCA 1989

FRIDAY 28TH APRIL, 1989
THE DUKE ARRIVED BY
HELICOPTER TO PLANT A TREE
IN THE QUADRANGLE,
AND UNVEIL
COMMEMORATING PLAQUES
IN HENRY GOTCH INFANT
AND JUNIOR SCHOOLS

THE HALL, DUKE'S VISIT, 1989

THE DUKE'S SPEECH, 1989

STAFF, DUKE'S VISIT, 1989

INFANTS QUADRANGLE, 1989

50TH CELEBRATION CAKE

INFANT STAFF WITH TREE DUKE PLANTED, 1989

TREE PLANTED BY DUKE, 1989

A ROYAL BIRTHDAY!

By Post Reporter

HENRY Gotch School's golden jubilee celebrations were given the Royal seal of approval last week.

Excited pupils and teachers watched as the Duke of Gloucester arrived by a helicopter of the Royal Flight on the school's playing field, to help the junior and infant schools celebrate 50 years of education.

Smiling

The smiling Duke was led into the hall of the junior school and a special assembly where the children sang a song written to mark the anniversary and he was presented with a picture, by Claire Brimley, made by pupils.

He also saw an exhibition of mementos and souvenirs from the school's 50 years, shown around by fourth year pupils, Sarah Walpole and Justin Caulfield.

In the neighbouring infants school there was another assembly and special songs from the children and the Duke went on to plant a tree in the school's quadrangle.

The Duke, who revealed he knows Kettering quite well, and often comes to shop in the town, told the pupils: "You should be very grateful for your school, there are many in the world that don't have the facilities you do."

● Top, Sarah Walpole and Justin Caulfield show the Duke the special exhibition, right, the Duke plants a commemorative tree watched by pupils fro the infants school.

Children at a Kettering school celebrating its golden jubilee te

Sharing our new school

by KRISTINE CHAPMAN

Henry Gotch Council School is now sharing with a London school.

News of the evacuees came early on the morning of 31 August. At about 2pm the billeting officers and helpers came to pack bags. Then, at 4.15, the school was closed to be made into a billeting centre.

On September 1st, 2nd and 3rd, evacuees from London were distributed from the school. On 13th September, the school re-opened and Mr Nobbs and Mrs Lightman, the headteachers of the evacuated school, visited Henry Gotch.

On the 21st, a two shift system started, Henry Gotch having the morning session from 8.30 to 12.30 and the Hall and fields from 2.15 to 3.15, and the London school having the afternoon session.

● YOUNG AUTHORS. . . Wayne Feast, Christopher Rose, Lauren Cox, Claire Brimley, Zoe Jones, Kristine Chapman, Daniel Barry, Emma McDonald and Victoria Earl at Henry Gotch Junior School.

EVENING TELEGRAPH ARTICLE, 1989

Senior School Magazine, 1989

19

MORE REFLECTIONS

I have been reflecting a lot lately - mainly due to another
Training course I am on at present - and not having been a
school teacher all my working life - i tried to remember the very
first school lesson I taught. It was here at Henry Gotch.

Coming from the gentle civilised (??) world of Commerce and
then FE, I regarded the invitation in 1985 from the head here, to
take a group of ("nice bunch" - I recall the words) fifth formers
for their final year of Commerce as an opportunity to widen my
teaching experience. After all, fifth years are, I thought, just
like I was (not so many years ago!) - decent hard-working,
sensible, ambitious and highly motivated (was I REALLY all of
those?) - AREN'T THEY??????? They just need treating like adults
- yes, I decided - treat them like adults, and they'll behave
like adults! WON'T THEY??

Armed with this comforting thought, I happily entered the (very
run down ex-cookery) classroom for the first timeto meet them. I
was greeted, with .... flying chalk,flying paper,
flying pencils, flying rubbers, flying something I care (nor dar)
not put a description on - and a board rubber that flew across,
narrowly missing my left ear. - not to mention the vivid-blue
language. I looked around ... and saw .. sixteen .. monsters -
sorry pupils ...... I think!! All the strange question looks I
had had from my FE colleagues when announcing my new "post"
Suddenly bore very distinct answers. I must be MAD! Resisting the
temptation to RUN I put down the armsful of papers etc I had been
hugging. I wondered what had happened to their previous teacher
who "had left". Rather late in the day I wished I had questioned
this more fully!

I took a check on myself. Well, I'm meant to be a school
teacher - so I'd better act like one (I tried to remember MY
school teachers!) - so, ... " I said , fairly loudly - in
my school teacher voice - which had no effect whatsoever -
repeated - a little louder - this time one or two students
looked at me with one eye .... finally I SHOUT (I vowed NEVER
to shout in a classroom!)
"PLEASE - (hopefully, saying an inward prayer) ......BE QUIET -
JUST FOR A MINUTE!" ---
SILENCE *****
Is shouting all they understand??
Suddenly, they notice me!
"She's new!" "Are you new,Miss?" "She's a bit young!" "She
won't last long!" "Who's she?" "Wot's she 'ere for?" "'Ere
Miss, are you our new teacher?"
"Yes" (a bit mouse-like) "cough" "Yes" (louder - more
confident!) "I'm Mrs. Blowman".
"Hey, you've got my shoes on, Miss!" exclaimed a voice at the
back, "where did you get them?" "Miss Selfridge, Miss?" "Like
your skirt,Miss" "Made it." "Wow! You can help me to sew!"
etc., etc., etc.
Suddenly the classroom was warm and friendly, the students, no
longer mean eyed objects - they were people - young people - who
fortunately felt they had something in common with me! (Even if
it was only that it was OK to shop at Miss Selfridge!)
We spent the first lesson chatting - not about Commerce - more
about boy-friends, fashion, music and a hundred and one things
(Yes, they were all girls!) I was getting to know them!

MRS BLOWMAN'S CONTRIBUTION TO 'CHALK FACE', 1989

NORTHAMPTONSHIRE COUNTY SCHOOLS' UNDER 14s

v

NOTTINGHAM FOREST F.C. UNDER 14s

Sunday, 14th May, 1989

Kick Off at 11.00 a.m.

BLISWORTH FOOTBALL CLUB (with kind permission)

COUNTY SCHOOLS, 1989

BhS
SCHOOL SOCCER
CHALLENGE

MATCH
PROGRAMME

NORTHAMPTONSHIRE COUNTY SCHOOLS' UNDER 14s

v

NOTTINGHAM FOREST F.C. UNDER 14s

Sunday, 14th May, 1989
Kick Off at 11.00 a.m.

BLISWORTH FOOTBALL CLUB (with kind permission)

NORTHAMPTONSHIRE UNDER 14s
(Silver and Royal Blue)

G.K.	Stuart Knight	N.S.B.
2.	Craig Adams	Kingsthorpe
3.	Chris Walton	Beanfield
4.	Chris Keay	Duston
5.	Graham Hillyer	Kingsthorpe
6.	Robin Sellers	Henry Gotch
7.	Ian King	Daventry
8.	Paul Lamb	N.S.B.
9.	Garry Harrison	Daventry
10.	Martin Aldridge	Grange
11.	Liam Heffernan	Thomas Beeket

Subs:

G.K.	Nathan Heads	Latimer
12.	Simon Stancomb	N.S.B.
14.	Scott Reid	Kingswood
15.	Ian Willis	N.S.B.

HENRY GOTCH INFANTS STAFF, 1990

MRS HOOPER, DEPUTY HEAD, INFANTS, CIRCA 1990

INFANT QUADRANGLE, 1990

1990

Parents in road demo

DRIVERS had to be patient this week as parents and children demonstrated in a series of protests to highlight a dangerous road in Kettering.

More than 70 parents and children demonstrated outside Henry Gotch School, Deeble Road, on Monday, in a bid to get a crossing. They vowed to continue their protest every morning this week.

On August 30, this year the Citizen reported that feeling among parents was growing and that they wanted improved saftey on the road.

At that time, Brian Harrison, chairman of the friends of Henry Gotch Infants School and Nursery Unit said many parents would be prepared to take direct action. Now Mr Harrison said he hoped the protest would get something done.

He said: "When we talk about children's safety we seem to be a little bit laid back. Until the unspeakable happens nobody really wants to do anything about it. We are not prepared to do so."

Mr Harrison said he wished to thank drivers for being patient and hoped the week-long protest would help in the battle for a pelican crossing.

He questioned the need for the new pelican crossing opposite shops on Windmill Avenue, arguing that the need for one on Deeble Road, was just as great.

(Photo:NV7058.7A)

SCHOOL SECRETARY, MAUREEN LIGGINS, CIRCA 1990

HENRY GOTCH INFANTS STAFF, 1991

HENRY GOTCH INFANTS PUPILS, 1991

ANNE ASQUITY-ELLIS, HEAD (INFANTS) & GOVERNORS, HEALTH AWARD, CIRCA 1992

HENRY GOTCH INFANTS STAFF, 1992

Ark is all in name of art

ANIMALS go in two by two at a Kettering infants school — thanks to this superb mural of Noah's Ark.

Children at Henry Gotch Infants School, Windmill Avenue, and their parents have been brushing up on the biblical tale.

Work started in September last year and finished earlier this year after 60 hours of painting and ten tins of different coloured paint.

Keen painters added more to the mural each Saturday morning, much to the amazement of the pupils who couldn't wait to go to school on Mondays and see the work.

Teacher and designer Amanda Brewin said: "It really has brightened up a rather grim wall. The children have been watching it grow stage by stage."

Pictured saluting the work are, from left, Ryan Andrews, Chloe MacAllister, Martin Cooper, twins Gary and Rebecca Thornton and Richard Elliott.

ET picture: MR17926.5A

CIRCA 1992

MRS BITHRAY, CHRISTMAS PARTY, CIRCA 1992

INFANTS CHRISTMAS PARTY, 1992

HENRY GOTCH INFANTS PUPILS, 1992

INFANTS CHRISTMAS PLAY, 1992

DAVID BLAIR, INFANTS TEACHER, CIRCA 1992

JUNIOR SCHOOL SWIMMING GALA, CIRCA 1992

JUNIOR SCHOOL BARBECUE, CIRCA 1992

John is top of his class

OHN Toon chalked up a first for Henry Gotch unior School, Kettering, when he was named 'eacher of the Year by local radio station KCBC.

John, pictured above, was nominated for his 'brillance' and 'understanding' by 25 pupils from class Six. He was presented with a cup by ester Cowling, chairman of the radio station.

Nominations for the award came from pupils, parents, school governors and colleagues at schools in Wellingborough, Corby and Kettering. The aim was to discover a teacher's special achievement or quality.

A surprised John exclaimed: "I'm absolutely peechless and over the moon! It is good to know he work I'm doing is being appreciated. But I ive all credit to the kids for their feedback.

"They throw themselves into everything — even when I announce it is a dreaded maths lesson, they respond with enthusiasm! They are the best class I've ever had."

Lester said KCBC wanted to draw attention to the importance of good teachers. He hoped the award would become an annual event.

CIRCA 1992

Sir splashes out

OOL it! Teacher David Drew plashed out in the sunshine yesteray.

Mr Drew, in charge of PE, needed o invitation to test the water as the ountry sizzled in the heat.

It was to celebrate Henry Gotch

Junior School opening its pool for the first time since 1990.

Head Peter Mayles said all 222 pupils will be making full use of the pool which was out of action last year because of repairs.

ET picture: MY18916.1

MAY 1992

INFANTS, CIRCA 1993

JUNIORS MAYPOLE REHEARSAL, CIRCA 1992

MRS FISKE, OPERATION SPRINGCLEAN, CIRCA 1994

20ᵀᴴ March 1994
£2,000 worth of
computer equipment is
stolen from the school.

MRS PHILLIPS, OPERATION SPRINGCLEAN,
CIRCA 1994

INFANT HEAD ANNE ASQUITH-ELLIS,
CIRCA 1993

KATHY Loveridge, right, is retiring after 20 years teaching at a Kettering school.

Staff and pupils at Henry Gotch Junior School, in Windmill Avenue, will hold a special assembly today for Mrs Loveridge, 50.

She has taught seven and eight year olds for several years and was also the school's science teacher.

Headteacher Peter Mayles said: "She has been a great asset to the school and has a highly professional manner.

"She is the school's longest serving teacher and is now teaching the children of some of her past pupils."

ET picture: CJL60271.4

JUNIORS, CIRCA 1995

INFANTS & NURSERY STAFF, CIRCA 1995

HENRY GOTCH
JUNIOR SCHOOL
KETTERING
1995
CLASS 1

HENRY GOTCH
JUNIOR SCHOOL
KETTERING
1995
CLASS 2

HENRY GOTCH
JUNIOR SCHOOL
KETTERING
1995
CLASS 3

HENRY GOTCH
JUNIOR SCHOOL
KETTERING
1995
CLASS 4

HENRY GOTCH
JUNIOR SCHOOL
KETTERING
1995
CLASS 5

HENRY GOTCH
JUNIOR SCHOOL
KETTERING
1995
CLASS 6

HENRY GOTCH
JUNIOR SCHOOL
KETTERING
1995
CLASS 7

HENRY GOTCH
JUNIOR SCHOOL
KETTERING
1995
CLASS 8

A helping of smiles for Carole

SCHOOL dinner supervisor Carole Humphrey was given a huge send-off by children and staff.

Mrs Humphrey started work at Henry Gotch Infants School in Kettering in 1975 and has seen many changes.

She said: "When I started the school still had hot dinners and a canteen.

"I will miss the children because I've spent a lot of time looking after them and I have got to know them quite well. Some of them can be little humbugs sometimes but most of the time they are lovely."

Mrs Humphrey's husband Brian, a company accountant, is also retiring and the couple are looking forward to several holidays they have lined up.

They are also expecting to be kept busy with their first grandchild, due in September.

But Mrs Humphrey is not saying goodbye to the school entirely because she will be going back occasionally on a voluntary basis.

‑ Carole Humphrey receives best wishes from pupils, from left Benjamin Tyndall, Kieron Johnson, ..y, Savanna Pedro and Jessica Kinchin

ET picture:CAP13855.14

CIRCA 1996

MRS FISKE TEACHING, CIRCA 1996

Year 5 1996
visiting
The Big Pit
In Govilon

2nd September 1996
Mrs Greaves and
Mrs Fothergill
start work

NATIONAL COAL BOARD
SOUTH WESTERN DIVISION
BIG PIT
COLLIERY

HENRY GOTCH SECONDARY MODERN, 1996

HENRY GOTCH SENIORS, 1996

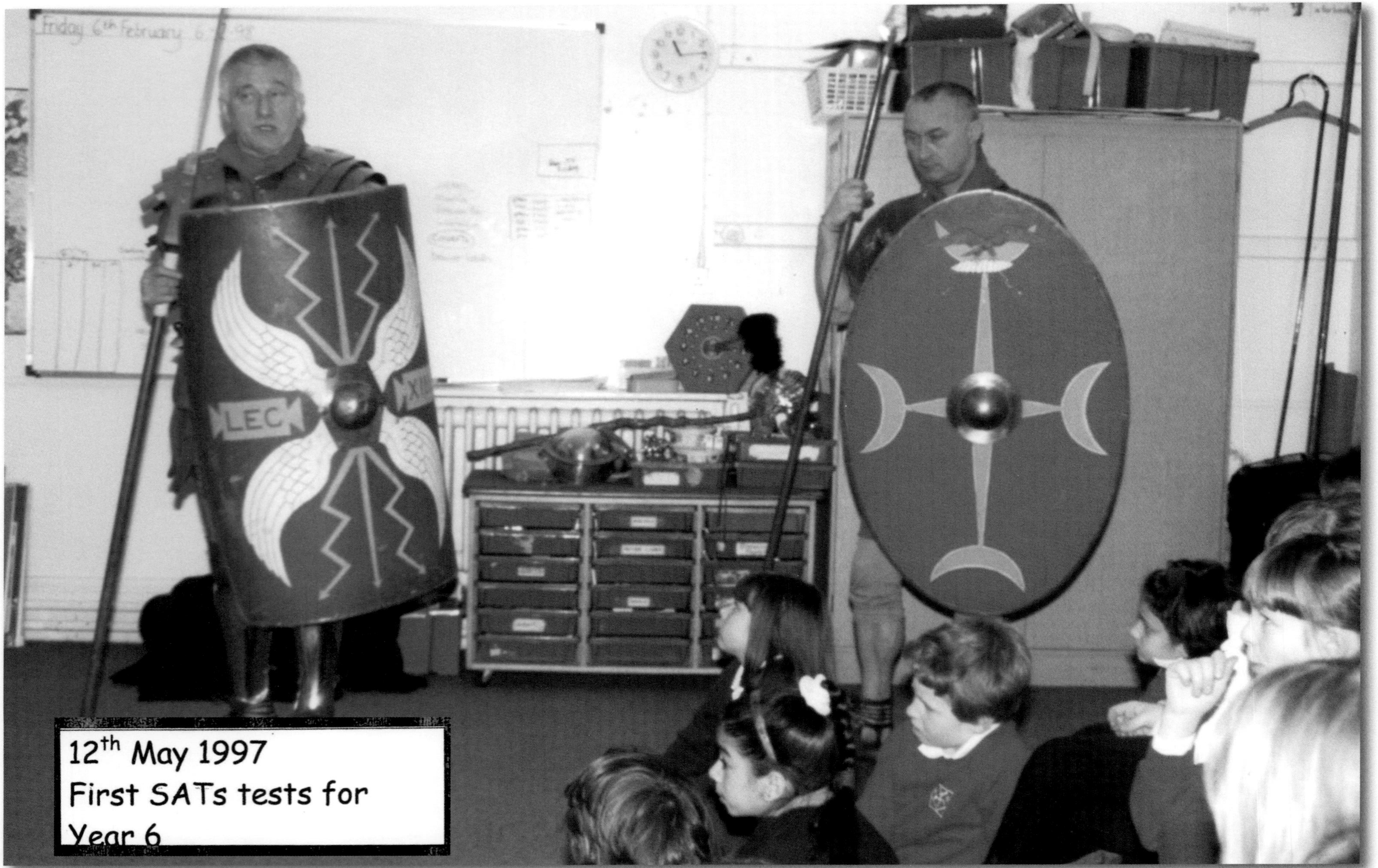
Friday 6th February
LEC
12th May 1997
First SATs tests for
Year 6

ROMAN SOLDIERS VISIT, CIRCA 1997

THE BOYS, CIRCA 1997

MRS SHERKELS CLASS, 1997

DINNER LADIES, 1997

MRS FISKE & MRS SOUTHWELL, INFANT TEACHERS, CIRCA 1998

FORMER HEAD, MR MAYLES, CIRCA 1998

INFANT PLAYTIME, CIRCA 1999

CIRCA 1999

STRICT DISCIPLINARIAN, MR DREW,
VICTORIAN DAY, 1999

MRS TATTERSALL,
VICTORIAN DAY (ADDINGTON), 1999

CICA

SUPER SCHOOLS

CERTIFICATE

AWARDED IN RECOGNITION OF EFFORT AND
ACHIEVEMENT IN THE CICA SUPERSCHOOLS
SPONSORED EXERCISES

FOR SUPERSCHOOLS

Brian Hooper

BRIAN HOOPER
WORLD SUPERSTARS
CHAMPION

FOR CICA

DAVID HARDING
DIRECTOR

HENRY GOTCH SCHOOL, YEAR 11, 1999

Henry Gotch Secondary Modern School ceased to exist when, on the 1st September 2000 following consultation and a decision by the Governors in June of the same year, its name was changed to Ise Community College.

The Student roll now numbers 985 and by 2007 this will have risen to over 1,200. There is a total staff of 98, including 63 teachers and 35 support staff. There are 35 form groups in the compulsory schooling age range and around 115 students in the 6th Form.

It all seems a very far cry from the 1950s.

ISE COMMUNITY COLLEGE
OUR MISSION

Ise Community College seeks to provide a centre of excellence in which individuals are encouraged to develop to the full.

OUR AIMS

HIGH EXPECTATIONS
To encourage positive responsible attitudes, respect and self discipline in a learning community which takes pride in hard work and high standards of achievement.

RELEVANT EDUCATION
To give all Students equal opportunity to enjoy a high quality, balanced learning experience which meets their needs in our rapidly developing world.

QUALITY LEARNING ENVIRONMENT
To provide a safe, secure ad caring environment in which high quality staff can encourage all to do their best.

SUPPORTIVE PARTNERSHIP
To work in a partnership with parents and the wider community which values every individual and provides both the support and challenge to achieve excellence.

CELEBRATION OF SUCCESS
To value and celebrate all achievements, taking pride in the personal development of individuals and the success of the whole school community.

Henry Gotch Primary School

Windmill Avenue, Kettering, Northamptonshire, NN15 7EA.
Email: bursar@henrygotch-pri.northants-ecl.gov.uk   Headteacher: Mrs. Liz Smorfitt B.Ed.
Tel: 01536 513088   Fax: 01536 411961

Dear Parent/Carer

Spring Term 1 – Newsletter

Spring Term One has certainly been busy if not a little disjointed, in terms of significant events. First there was the HMI monitoring visit (you should have all received a copy by now), then we had the snow fiasco and consequent closure, and finally we took the decision to defer the residential visit for Year 4. We will obviously keep you advised of how we intend to re-schedule the visit, but I know everyone was disappointed at not being able to go. However, the snow was great and I'm sure the children will have many happy memories of building snowmen and having fun.

Assessment of Pupils' Progress

We have just completed our third assessment week and the children's results show definite signs of improvement, in some cases very good progress. However, we are half way through the year and several children need to apply themselves more fully to their work if they hope to make good progress. Please would you ensure that your children read for a short period at home every night (15 mins will do fine) and that they complete any homework given. Also, it is very important that children attend school every day; poor attendance links directly to inadequate academic progress, so it is vital that children have access to the curriculum opportunities provided.

Staffing

I have already written to specific classes to update parents on arrangements for their children. We work constantly to try and create stability but, as you know, we do experience periods when staff are unwell.

I need to advise you that Mr Lenton will be leaving us at the end of February; he has decided to pursue a career in the music industry. Mr Lenton has been here for some years, working in class and on the football field with the children. We all wish him well and we thank him for all his contributions to the life of the school.

Former Staff

I received news this week that Joyce Peasley, a former Headteacher of the Infants' School, died suddenly recently at her home. Mrs Peasley was the Headteacher from 1959 – 1965. I don't know if any of your families were pupils then, I understand the local press intend to publish an article about her soon. The funeral service will be held at The Albert Munn Chapel, of Kettering Crematorium, on Monday February 16th at 12.25pm.

Learning and Growing Together

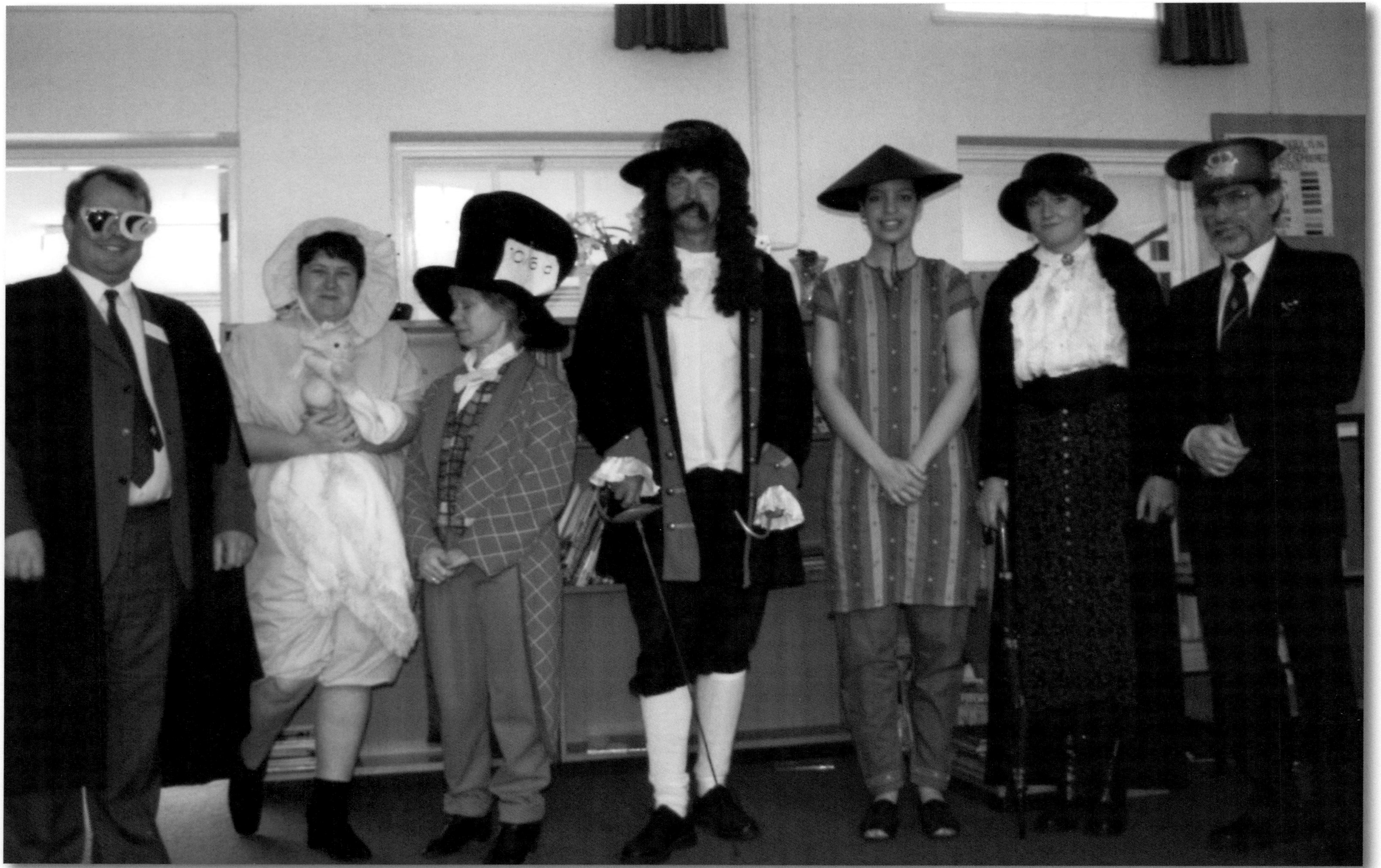

JUNIOR SCHOOL, WORLD BOOK DAY, CIRCA 2001

FARYL SMITH, YEAR 3, NOMINATES MR TOON AS TEACHER OF THE YEAR, 2002

CHARLOTTE PREPARING FOR HER
FIRST DAY AT SCHOOL, 2003

TRADITIONAL CHRISTMAS DECORATIONS
INFANTS & JUNIORS

■ **BLAZE AFTERMATH** – the scene at Henry Gotch Junior School this morning

ET picture: 080404.8.3

Arsonists blamed for school blaze

BY MARTIN ROBINSON

ARSONISTS are thought to be behind a fire that threatened to rip through a school early today.

Fire crews were called at 2am after the fire broke out in a boiler room at Henry Gotch Junior School in Deeble Road, Kettering, and smoke was seen billowing from the building.

The flames were brought under control within three hours and firefighters managed to limit the damage to the basement, which suffered severe water damage.

No-one was injured.

Investigators have already ruled out electrical or mechanical faults as the cause of the fire.

Headteacher Heather Donoyou said: "We have decided to close the school today after the fire. I would like to reiterate that the building is completely safe; we just have no heating at present.

"At the moment we are unsure whether the school will be open on Monday. We will contact parents with news.

"I would really like to thank all the parents for their help. All have passed on messages and have helped us so much on this difficult day."

Parent Carol Ingram, of Ise Lodge, Kettering, was shocked to see what had happened and relieved that no-one was injured.

She said: "My husband heard it on the radio but it did not say it was closed.

"I called the school at 8am but there was no answer. I have literally just arrived and seen it is closed. I just hope everyone is OK."

The school is planning a clean-up operation today and over the weekend.

It is hoped that the school will be open as normal on Monday morning.

Henry Gotch Junior School

PEDESTRIAN ENTRANCE

JUNIOR SCHOOL CLOSED TODAY DUE TO FIRE

CIRCA 2003

SPECIAL PERFORMANCE FOR ONE NIGHT ONLY
PATRICK FLATLEY
King of the Irish Dancers

DAILY MIRROR....
"Patrick..
Lord of the
Dance"

BILLY LIAR
He's the
Greatest since
Cassius Clay.
Patrick Flatly
Reigns

THE STAR...
Opportunity
"Knocks" for
Patrick

DAILY EXPRESS...
A Great
Performance !

DAILY MAIL...
The Pop Idol
of
Dancing..

THE SUN...
Not to be
Missed....

Special Admission Price: we pay you 5p to attend
OAP's concessions

FORMER HENRY GOTCH PUPIL, RICHARD (PAT) FEARNE, MADE A BID FOR INTERNATIONAL
STARDOM AT THE 'RIVEIRA' WEYMOUTH, 2003. IT WAS HIS FIRST AND LAST APPEARANCE

1ST INTAKE OPENING OF SENIOR SCHOOL 1953, 50 YEARS RE-UNION, 1953–2003

INFANT CLASS, 2004

Children transform garden

CHILDREN have turned a teacher's memorial garden into a touchy-feely haven of smells, colour and sounds.

The raised garden at Henry Gotch Infants School, in Kettering, was created in memory of teacher Irene Bailey who died of cancer.

Planted more than ten years ago, pupils and teachers decided it lacked colour and wanted to spruce it up.

Now, thanks to the hard work of the school's five and six-year-olds, it is bursting with life and has a water feature, pottery animals and musical pipes.

Herbs that give off scents have also been planted to create a truly sensual experience.

Class teaching assistant Jane Hughes said the children designed and planted the garden and will continue to water and weed it.

She said: "They have really enjoyed it and have been so enthusiastic."

■ GROWING BEAUTIFULLY – teacher Jane Hughes with, from left, Nicole Johnson, six, Justine Garcia, six, Kyle McAlwane, five, Stefan Constable, six, Lauren Fuins, six, and Chloe Wilson, six

ET picture by Glyn Dobbs: 180705.4.1

2005

VISIT TO DUXFORD, STAFF DRESS UP AS EVACUEES, CIRCA 2005

IRENE BAILEY'S (LATE) GARDEN TENDED BY CHILDREN OF
HINWICK HALL WITH MRS DREDGE

Former pupils do the honours

Opening of school's £750,000 extension

By Martin Robinson

FORMER pupils of a primary school were invited back to perform a very special duty – opening its £750,000 extension.

Maureen Liggins and John Sellers cut the ribbon at the new block at Henry Gotch Primary School in Kettering.

Mrs Liggins attended the school in 1939, her children went there and she was also school secretary for 30 years.

Mr Sellers is one of the school's well-known former pupils, after he wrote his successful book Adventures of a Henry Gotch Boy in 2005.

Mrs Liggins said: "It is a wonderful building and really well designed.

"The school has changed since I was here as a pupil and from a former secretary's perspective it would also be a dream to work in a place like this. There is so much room."

The extension at the school in Deeble Road includes a new staff room, reception officer, school office, headteacher's office and other vibrant rooms for staff and pupils to enjoy.

Headteacher Heather Donoyou said: "This is a fantastic facility, which gives us much more room to work in.

"In particular there is an advantage for our teaching staff, as before we had no specific space set aside for them to deal with their paperwork.

"The building also links the two old buildings, which since the junior and infants schools joined, makes for a unified feel.

"We are proud and delighted with the block and the financial support we have received from

Northamptonshire County Council.

Year 5 pupil Adam Cattell also likes the building's architecture and internal design. He said: "I like the multi-coloured carpets and the big windows. It makes the school a nicer place to be. It is brilliant."

MRS LIGGINS & JOHN SELLERS, OPENING OF NEW BUILDING, 2005

NEW ANNEXE SHOWING RAINBOW CARPET, 2005

NEW STAFF ROOM, 2005

SECRETARY ANITA STOKES IN NEW OFFICE
WITH COMMEMORATIVE STONE

JAMIE RALPH MEMORIAL CHAIR, 2005

In loving memory
of
Jamie Ralph
a dearly loved and special
friend and pupil at
Henry Gotch Junior School
September 2001 – June 2005

JAMIE RALPH MEMORIAL PLAQUE, 2005

JAMIE'S TROPHY

INFANTS, 2006

HENRY GOTCH PRIMARY, 2006

Gold Award

Presented to........... Charlotte Curie ....

Date..... 6. 7. 07 ....

For the outstanding achievement of 40 merits

HENRY GOTCH PRIMARY, 2007

INFANT CLASSWORK, 2008

A smile...................

A smile is infectious; you catch it like the flu,
When someone smiled at me today, I started smiling too.
I passed around the corner and someone saw my grin
When they smiled I realised I had passed it on to them.

I thought about that smile, then I realised as with
A single smile, just like mine could travel round the earth.
So, if you feel a smile beginning, don't leave it undetected.
Let's start an epidemic quick, and get the world infected!!!

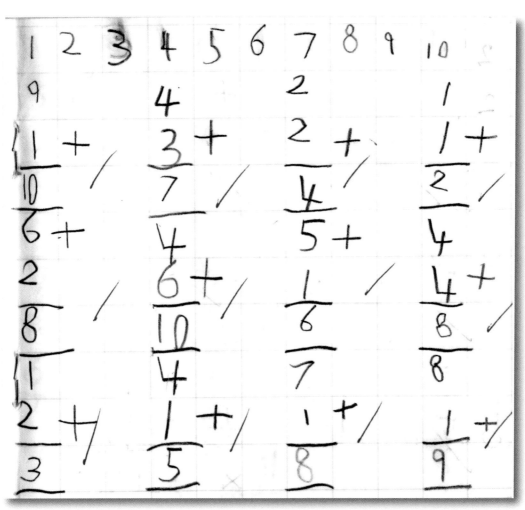

1 2 3 4 5 6 7 8 9 10

9		4			2		1

1 +   3 +   2 +   1 +
—   —   —   —
10 /   7 /   4 /   2 /

6 +   4   5 +   4 +
—   6 +   —   4 +
2 /   —   1 /   8
           10 /   6   —
                      —   8
8   4   7
—   —
1   1 +   1 +   1 +
2 +   5   8 /   9
—   —   —   —
3   5   8
2

INFANT MATHS, 2008

Thursday
January 26th

9		4		6		2

1 +   3 +   3 +   1 +
—   —   —   —
10 /   7 /   9 /   3 /

6   4   4 +   4

2 +   6 +   2 +   6 +
—   —   —   —
     /   10 /   6 /   6

2 +   4 +   4 +   6 +
—   —   —   —
     /   5   6   9   3

Schools axed as academy gets go-ahead

■ By Bernie Goodjohn

bernie.goodjohn@northantsnews.co.uk

PLANS to close two schools and create a new academy have been given the final go-ahead.

Northamptonshire County Council's cabinet yesterday voted unanimously to close Ise Community College and Henry Gotch School in Kettering to make way for the academy, which will be one of two in the town.

Cllr Joan Kirkbride, cabinet member for children and young people, said the academy plans had the approval of people in the community.

The schools will officially close at the end of the school year on August 31 and the academy will open on September 1.

CONTACT US

Do you think the academy will improve standards? Let us know by:
■ Emailing editor.et
@northantsnews.co.uk

It will cater for pupils from four to 18 and the Brooke Weston Trust will sponsor the academy, as confirmed last year.

It will specialise in science, business and enterprise.

By closing the two schools and creating the academy, the county council hopes to see an improvement in levels of achievement.

A public consultation on the academy proposals was carried out last year and Cllr Kirkbride issued statutory notices for the closure of the schools in January.

In a council report outlining the closure proposal, she said the expected benefit of creating the academy would be the "impact on performance indicators".

She said: "This will be an improvement in achievement levels in the schools involved and on school performance."

Ise Community College is a National Challenge School, which means it is on a programme to help improve standards, and Henry Gotch Primary School is in the Ofsted notice to improve category.

Last month, plans to close Montagu School and Avondale infants and junior schools in Kettering to create another academy were also approved.

That academy, which is being sponsored by the United Learning Trust, will be called Kettering Buccleuch Academy and it is also set to open in September.

Henry Gotch Primary School
Celebrates
70 Years

Henry Gotch Primary School, formerly Henry Gotch Nursery/Infant/Junior School is celebrating its

70th Anniversary Year this summer.

It will be closing in its present form on 31st August 2009.
The School will be merging with ISE Community College to become Kettering Science Academy on 1st September 2009.

We would like to take this opportunity to invite
Former Staff and Governors to the School Open Days on:

Tuesday 7th July 2009
Friday 10th July 2009

10.00 – 2.30pm

We hope that you can attend and we look forward to your taking a trip down Memory Lane
Please contact the school office if you would like to attend 01536 513088

2009

CARETAKER'S HOUSE

PETER MCGLYN, LAST CARETAKER (SITE SUPERVISOR)

MILLENNIUM GARDEN
WE DID IT, WHEN WE B&Q'd IT

MR & MRS JOHNSON, CARETAKERS, 26 YEARS

MISS MOLLY COOKE, INFANT TEACHER, 1955, FORMER PUPILS,
DAVID ROBINSON (LEFT) AND AUTHOR JOHN SELLERS (RIGHT)
2009

JOHN SELLERS, AUTHOR, LAST DAY 2009

HENRY GOTCH
70TH
ANNIVERSARY

VISITORS
BOOK

Comments and
memories

MRS FOTHERGILL WITH HER HOMEMADE 70TH ANNIVERSARY CAKE

MRS FOTHERGILL, FARYL SMITH & MR TOON, FINAL DAY

NURSERY SCHOOL, JULY 2009

INFANT SCHOOL HALL, JULY 2009

INFANT SCHOOL, JULY 2009

HENRY GOTCH PRIMARY STAFF, LAST DAY, JULY 2009

JUNIOR SCHOOL INTERIOR, 2009
CHANGED LITTLE OVER THE YEARS

PUPILS COME OUT TO PLAY FOR THE VERY LAST TIME, JULY 2009

JUNIOR SCHOOL, 2009

JUNIOR SCHOOL, JULY 2009

WORK BEGINS ON THE NEW ACADEMY, NOVEMBER 2010
"OH THOSE LOVELY MEMORIES OF THE SCHOOL PLAYING FIELDS"

WORK PROGRESSES, FEBRUARY 2011

NEW ACADEMY BUILDING

Kettering Science Academy's new £26m building is taking shape after work got under way in September. The new building for secondary pupils, which will replace the existing one, is due to open in September 2012.

The site on Deeble road has been a hive of activity and work has already started on laying the foundations of the impressive building, which will feature two 'super' science labs, a 450-seat theatre and classrooms with a glass wall for visibility. Sports facilities will include 'rubber-crumb' 5-a-side pitches, a sand-based artificial turf pitch and netball and tennis courts. KSA's sports facilities, along with its music, technology and drama departments, will be accessible for community use during the evenings, weekends and holidays. In addition, the IT facilities will enable community learning courses to be held at the Academy.

It is set to be the greenest building ever built in the county, with an underground heating system, the use of solar energy and data screens that will display the energy usage of the building.

KSA is part of the Brooke Weston Partnership, which already includes Brooke Weston Academy and Corby Business Academy. Specialist staff from the Partnership have been working with Northamptonshire County Council and contractors Willmott Dixon to ensure KSA's new building matches the high standards already evident at the other Partnership Academies. The existing Primary building will not miss out, with extensive refurbishment to the building and grounds planned.

Pupils and families are invited to find out more at a Sixth Form Open Evening on Tuesday, February 15th, starting at 6pm. Year 11 students will be able to find out what is on offer at KSA – including a new apprenticeship scheme in electrical installation - and discuss their options with subject leaders. Download the Sixth Form prospectus from the Academy's website, www.ketteringscienceacademy.org, or call the office on 01536 532700.

DEEBLE RD

WINDMILL AVE

NEW ACADEMY

Adventures of a
HENRY GOTCH
BOY

John Sellers